# A CENTURY OF CULTIVATION

## 1911 – 2011

### 100 YEARS FROM THE PENNSYLVANIA SCHOOL OF HORTICULTURE FOR WOMEN TO TEMPLE UNIVERSITY AMBLER

BY JENNY ROSE CAREY '03 & MARY ANNE BLAIR FRY '58
DIRECTOR, AMBLER ARBORETUM      ALUMNUS, PSHW & TEMPLE U.ED

OUR SINCERE GRATITUDE TO THE MANY STUDENTS AND GRADUATES THROUGH THE YEARS WHO TOOK THE TIME AND INTEREST TO PRODUCE THE SCHOOL PUBLICATIONS. GENUINE THANKS TO ALL THE ALUMNI WHO OVER THE YEARS TOOK THE TIME TO WRITE INTO THE ALUMNI ASSOCIATION WITH THEIR NEWS OF FAMILY AND CAREERS. WITHOUT THESE PUBLICATIONS FOR OUR RESEARCH, WE WOULD NOT HAVE BEEN ABLE TO ASSEMBLE THIS HISTORY OF OUR BELOVED SCHOOL AND ITS ESTEEMED GRADUATES.

PENNSYLVANIA
SCHOOL OF
HORTICULTURE
FOR WOMEN

THIS CENTENNIAL BOOK IS A WORK OF LOVE BY A GROUP OF LOYAL AND
DEVOTED GRADUATES WHO FELT THE NEED TO RECORD THE REMEMBRANCES
AND DEVELOPMENTS OF THE SCHOOL OF HORTICULTURE AND
TEMPLE UNIVERSITY AMBLER.

WE WOULD LIKE TO THANK THE FOLLOWING CONTRIBUTORS FOR THEIR SUPPORT OF THIS PROJECT: *Gus & Jenny Rose Carey, Art Curtze, Betsy Spangler Evans, Mary Anne Blair Fry, Faith & Joseph Tiberio, Claire Weir Whiting and the School of Environmental Design Alumni Association.*

# Foreward

This year—2011—the *Pennsylvania School of Women* has turned 100. It is no longer known by that name, as *Temple University* took the reins in 1958—the year I graduated. Today, the title is *School of Environmental Design, College of Liberal Arts, Temple University*; referred to as *Temple University Ambler*. I have been 'attached' to this campus for 55 of those 100 years; intrigued and amazed by the stories of the lives and careers of my fellow graduates. Oral tradition is great, but our history was in danger of being lost as our older graduates were no longer with us and without a written record their stories would be forgotten. Information for the book was gleaned from several school journals: *Wise Acres*, *The Quarterly* and *Pen & Trowel*. Using the inspiration from Temple University's founder, Dr. Russell Conwell, and his book ACRES OF DIAMONDS, I gathered stories of outstanding graduates—our gems. The more I read and researched the more difficult it became to choose the 'Diamonds of the Decades', for we have so many that could be recognized. It is my hope that you will enjoy these stories and be inspired to record your own, by sending in notes of your accomplishments for our future records. I hope too, that this book will plant the seeds of remembrance in the minds of those who read it and continue to cultivate the careers of current and future graduates that the harvest of this amazing school will keep enriching our land.

—*Mary Anne Blair Fry '58*

# Introduction

This book contains one hundred years of history for a site that began as a novel idea in women's education and continues today as both a co-educational establishment and an arboretum.

The site at *Temple University Ambler* is a women's history site, with a state historic marker located on Meetinghouse Road. There are few women's history sites in Pennsylvania and we are proud of our heritage not only as the site of the innovative *Pennsylvania School of Horticulture for Women* (PSHW) in 1911, but also as the founding site of the *Woman's National Farm and Garden Association* (WNF&GA) in 1914.

The one hundred year history is chronicled in this book, decade by decade. Beginning with Jane Bowne Haines' vision for a new way to teach girls practical skills in America. Showing the growth and expansion of the school under the leadership of Louise Bush-Brown. Continuing with the ups and downs of the school during the changing social and economic conditions of the twentieth century and leading to the merger of the *School of Horticulture* with *Temple University*. The evolution and diversification of courses, the new buildings, each decade of the history has had its challenges and successes. The book concludes with images of those involved with *Temple University Ambler* today.

Most of the information in this book is from the *Temple University Ambler Archives* in the Ambler Library, and has not been published before. There is also a public display of artifacts in the Hilda Justice building, the old library. If you would like to know more about the site and the people who worked and studied here, please come visit—we have much to share with you.

—*Jenny Rose Carey '03*

# Contents

# School Song

O beautiful for meadows wide,
For fields of yellow corn,
For verdant woodland privacies
And crimson skies at dawn!
O Alma Mater! Ambler dear!
Our hymn to thee we raise,
In every place, God give His grace
To beautify thy ways.

O dearly loved for April days
For hours of toil and ease,
For beauties of thy garden ways
And music of thy bees!
O Alma Mater! Ambler dear!
We pledge our hearts to thee
And trust God's hand will let thee stand
Firm through the changing years!

O glorious for Autumn days
When rich thy harvest yields,
For beauties of thy western skies,
For winds that sweep thy fields!
O Alma Mater! Ambler dear!
God shed His light o'er thee
And give increase without surcease
And nobler let thee be!

Victorious for future days
When over all the earth,
Thy students bear thy lessons far
And nobly prove thy worth!
O Alma Mater! Ambler dear!
God bless thee ever more,
Thy name we sing, oh let it ring
From East to Western shore!

*Words by Louise Carter Bush-Brown '16*

"Our vision was of a place where earnest-minded women could live and dream, where they should not be expected to do household work, but should give their whole time to learning under competent teachers to become competent workers."

—Jane Bowne Haines

# CHAPTER 1: *Progressive Women*

## Jane Bowne Haines

On an April afternoon in the year 1910, Jane B. Haines presented to a congress of women at Bryn Mawr her plans for the founding of the first school of horticulture for women in America. Quoting from Miss Haines;

*"Believing thoroughly in the principle of horticultural training for women and that the time for founding such an institution is now come, a number of people have associated themselves together with the purpose of opening, in the near future, a school for this practical training of women in gardening and kindred subjects. The purpose of the school is to offer to educated and earnest minded women, who have a love for country life and an aptitude for country pursuits, practical training in horticulture... One principle above all others would we keep before us and would particularly enforce the trained hand with the trained mind, which means mastery and success."*

Born to an established Philadelphia Quaker family, Jane Bowne Haines grew up on her father's 100 acre estate in Cheltenham, PA. Horticulture was always a part of Jane's life. Her father owned a fruit and shade tree nursery, and her ancestor was Caspar Wistar, a well known horticulturist and amateur botanist. Jane learned the fundamentals of horticulture in the family's formal gardens at Wyck in Germantown, PA.

Jane graduated from Bryn Mawr College and attended library school in Albany, NY, which led to her employment with the Library of Congress. She later returned home to run the family nursery. It was then that she committed herself to the idea of founding a horticultural school for women. Through this school, she hoped to provide women with career education that would enable them to find employment opportunities beyond the usual educational or secretarial jobs offered to women at the time. She also wanted to impart more self confidence in the young women and allow them to realize and appreciate their own abilities. Reaching beyond the boundaries of her own school, Jane aspired that the *Pennsylvania School of Horticulture for Women* (PSHW) would not only educate women locally, but would also serve as a model for all forward-thinking, enterprising women across the nation.

**PHOTOGRAPHS:** (TOP LEFT) AN EARLY PORTRAIT OF JANE BOWNE HAINES, FROM A SCHOOL PROSPECTUS; (LEFT) STUDENTS IN WINTER UNIFORMS TILL THE FIELDS. **OPPOSITE PAGE:** (TOP) AN EARLY PHOTOGRAPH OF A PRUNING DEMONSTRATION IN THE APPLE ORCHARD; (BOTTOM LEFT) STUDENTS MAKING ROOT GRAFTS; (BOTTOM RIGHT) AN ADVERTISEMENT FOR THE SCHOOL FROM WISE ACRES, JUNE, 1914.

# A Modest Start

During the months preceding the delivery of Jane Bowne Haine's presentation at Bryn Mawr, a survey had been made of the European Colleges of Gardening, and a decision was made to establish this new school in America along similar lines. A small farm was purchased near what was then the little country town of Ambler. The first entry in the Log Book, which was kept during those early days, is dated September 21st, 1910; *"Work has begun on the alterations and repairs of the house."*

The farm house was converted into student and faculty dining rooms along with the kitchen and an office on the first floor. The second and third floors held the Director's office and private living quarters for the staff and maids. Work on the old farm house continued throughout the winter months and on February 10th, 1911, The Pennsylvania School of Horticulture for Women officially opened its doors with Miss Mary Collins as principal, Miss Varley as instructor, and four students.

By March 24th, 1911, the first greenhouse was completed and a small cottage served as a dormitory for eight students. According to Louise Carter '16; the *"classroom was the sun porch of the farm house; seating was a shelf of two pine boards which had been placed against the windows with our backs to the instructor who stood in the doorway."* Fortunately, founder of the school, Jane Bowne Haines, encouraged a *"learn by doing"* teaching method and education came not only from the classroom, but also through active work on the school grounds.

Classes were held Monday to Friday, from 7:30 in the morning until 5:30 in the evening. The students gained experience in a variety of areas including horticulture, botany, orchard care, gardening, livestock, bee keeping, poultry, chemistry, business, marketing, and even carpentry. As Jane Bowne Haines predicted, *"the first students in the school will have much of the fun, for to them will be given an insight into the foundation of things; the laying out and planting of the gardens and grounds, and the creating of custom and precedent so dear to all schools and colleges."*

In 1914, when Louise Carter enrolled she recalled there were only 14 students, *"four in the previous class and ten incoming students."* The first years were a learning experience for all and it was not until 1915 that the school held its first official commencement ceremony with three graduates.

**PHOTOGRAPHS:** (TOP LEFT) AN OLD POSTCARD OF THE ORIGINAL GREENHOUSE; (TOP RIGHT) WOMEN SHOVEL COMPOST AROUND THE COLD FRAMES; (RIGHT) JUNIOR CLASS, IN FRONT OF THE OLD FARMHOUSE DECEMBER, 1914.

"A large number of farmers and students from the Pennsylvania School of Horticulture were present to witness the demonstration—"breaking up of clay subsoil with dynamite."

—Ambler Gazette, April 20th, 1911

In 1912, the official school uniform consisted of a *"khaki suit for summer work and a brown corduroy suit for winter work,"* School Prospectus, 1912. In the cold months, women also wore heavy full length top coats. Within a few years the original uniform was replaced by sailor dresses, with "middy" (midshipman) collars, which were especially popular around the time of World War I. The "middy" dresses did not last long before they were replaced by, *"a Duxbak skirt of a length 10" inches or more from the ground; Ladies' Duxbak Norfolk jacket, hat, khaki or Duxbak, 'Asbury' style; shirt, khaki army flannel or khaki drill. High laced waterproof boots, golf stockings, and a tie,"* School Prospectus, 1919. For summer courses, the uniform was a simple one piece frock in brown or tan with similarly colored 'knickerbockers'. As restricting as these outfits may have been, they did not stop the women from climbing and pruning trees or blowing up the trees and subsoil with dynamite.

In December of 1914, thanks to the generosity of Mrs. Robert B. Haines, the mother of the Founder, the staff in the original administration building were able to enjoy the luxury of electric lights for the first time. The following year, the school's first new building was completed in April with a generous donation from Miss Emma Blakiston, who lived on the neighboring farm. This building held a classroom on the first floor and accommodation for faculty and students on the second and third floors. The move was long awaited and, on April 26th it was *"Moving day! With one accord and a Henry Ford we gaily made our long delayed entry into the new building..."* Wise Acres, March 1915. The classrooms occupied this building until 1960 and it is now the Administration Building for the Ambler campus with an addition added in 1976.

**PHOTOGRAPHS:** (TOP) BLASTING DEMONSTRATION BY MR. DOAN, 1911; (RIGHT) WINTER WORK IN THE NURSERY ROWS, FROM THE 1914 SCHOOL PROSPECTUS; (LEFT) WOMEN IN TOP COATS PRACTICE PRUNING THE GRAPE VINES.

In the autumn of 1915, Miss Edna Gunnel became the Head of Floriculture. Edna was a female graduate of the famous Kew Gardens training school outside of London. Although unsure of what to make of this English woman at first, the students quickly came to admire Miss Gunnel for her wealth of horticultural knowledge and expertise. Recalling Miss Gunnel's arrival on campus, Louise Carter mused: *"That evening after she had retired, we were intrigued to see a pair of shoes outside her door, where upon we hastily called a student conference. What should we do? Should we just leave them there, or should we polish them? At last someone suggested that we polish one of them and leave the other unpolished in order to get her used to it gradually. This, we decided, was a good solution. The shoes were never put out again."*

Another successful woman, Miss Elizabeth Leighton Lee, also began teaching at the school on February 2nd, 1915. Her specialty was Landscape Gardening. Miss Lee was among the first women in America to practice Landscape Architecture, and she was well known, which brought great distinction to the school. *"She had great dignity and personal charm and was deeply loved by the students."* Later in 1915, with the retirement of Jessie T. Morgan, Miss Lee took over as Director of the Pennsylvania School of Horticulture for Women.

Mr. John L. Doan, a graduate of Cornell and Purdue, also taught at PSHW in the early years. A strong supporter of women in agriculture, he wrote several articles for *Wise Acres* regarding the future of women in the field. When not writing articles for Wise Acres and other journals, he taught several courses, including one about 'Trees and Shrubs', which became infamous for the dynamite lessons in the apple orchard.

**PHOTOGRAPHS:** (TOP RIGHT) ELIZABETH LEIGHTON LEE, FROM WISE ACRES, 1927; (LEFT) CONSTRUCTION OF THE NEW GREENHOUSE, 1915; (BELOW) STUDENTS IN THE SCHOOL'S EARLY UNIFORM WORK IN THE GREENHOUSE.

In the early years of the school, the property comprised 71 acres, twenty acres of which contained crops for practice and demonstration work with students. These crops included an orchard, an asparagus plot, a vineyard of 250 vines, two acres of strawberries, and extensive flower and vegetable gardens, nurseries, a greenhouse, hot and cold frames, a model poultry plant, and a bee colony.

For as long as the school existed, so did the beehives, which were a valuable asset in many ways. In 1913, students gathered 400 pounds of strained honey, which they sold for 30 cents a pound. They also used the wax for hundreds of grafts and relied on the bees to fertilize their fruit trees. Later courses in beekeeping were taught by Miss Letitia E. Wright who covered topics such as the correct housing temperatures for honey production, honey collection methods, and even how to integrate a new Queen bee to a hive. As she noted in *Wise Acres*; *"combined with the raising of poultry or the growing of fruit, bees are a splendid investment."* In 1917, with the proceeds from the sale of the bees' products, the school built a bee house, which served to store the needed tools and as a canning space for the honey and wax.

When not busy in class or with work duties around the campus, the students often hosted visitors for teas and tours of the premises. Local train and trolley connections and the improved roads allowed for many day visitors, and in turn making it easier for the women to be visitors themselves at a multitude of surrounding farms and gardens, which were often the highlight of the women's experiences at PSHW over the years.

Edith Dornbrier '28 wrote: *"The field trips were valuable not only for the opportunities they offered us to observe applied horticulture, but also for their aesthetic value. What a thrill it was always to attend the big flower shows and to visit the beautiful estates around Philadelphia! And some of the most pleasant experiences I had were some of the little field trips organized by the students themselves during free time, sometimes just into the woods across the road and sometimes as far afield as the Jersey Marshes or the Poconos. Other treasured memories of the school are the social affairs planned for us by the faculty and Board members—trips to concerts, teas at their homes, garden parties and the delightful musicales we attended upon several occasions in homes in Rittenhouse Square. It made one feel a part of the community."* Helena Manley '39 also wrote, *"I consider the visits to very special gardens and estates real privileges and among the most inspiring activities."*

On May 27th, 1915, even the stage came to Ambler as the students starred in their own moving picture produced by the Pathe Moving Picture Company who *"Bore down upon us and wound up our reels to the tune of hoeing, raking and dynamiting,"* *Wise Acres*, June, 1915.

**PHOTOGRAPHS:** (TOP LEFT) STUDENTS TENDING THE STRAWBERRY FIELDS; (TOP RIGHT) THE BEE BOXES IN THE WINTER OF 1914; (RIGHT) ON OCTOBER 8TH, 1914, DIRECTOR JESSIE T. MORGAN TOOK THE STUDENTS TO A CONVENTION OF THE MARKET GROWERS ASSOCIATION OF AMERICA HELD AT HORTICULTURAL HALL, UPON ARRIVAL THEY WERE HELD UP BY A PHOTOGRAPHER EAGER TO PHOTOGRAPH THE LARGE GROUP OF FEMALE ATTENDEES.

During a meeting held at 2PM on January 12th, 1914, the eight students at the School of Horticulture for Women decided that a school paper would be *"a very nice thing"* and Miss Emily Exley became the first editor. The original layout was designed by Miss Francis Shin and was maintained in future editions of *Wise Acres*. Funding for the paper was obtained in part by the sale of advertising space as well as through an egg and vegetable route involving the school work horse, Prince, hitched to the *"jagger-wagon"* to carry the produce around town. This route became quite popular and the students often sold everything, with a portion of the profits retained for publication of *Wise Acres*.

Publications were initially kept to three times a year until the local post office agreed to extend "magazine rates" if *Wise Acres* were to be mailed out four times a year. After short discussion, the students decided the reduced mailing costs and additional advertising would be beneficial and thus a fourth publication was added.

Through *Wise Acres*, the students were also able to advertise the school wares—plants and seedlings, canned goods and food products, and various courses offered throughout the year. There were also "how to" articles, such as the one in the 1920 October edition of *Wise Acres* that described the winning protocol for *'washing a bird for show'* with interesting tips and debates on the use of blue dye or bleach versus a diet of white corn.

*Wise Acres* was temporarily suspended during WWI; quoting from the July, 1918 issue; *"Whereas the war in which our country is engaged makes every unnecessary use of paper, labor, and time an unpatriotic act and whereas the publication of Wise Acres involves such a use, be it resolved that the publication of Wise Acres be suspended indefinitely after the issue for July, 1918."* At the conclusion of the War, publication was re-initiated and continued to be printed through the fifties. In the 1940's, *Wise Acres* changed from a quarterly publication to the school yearbook.

---

CLIPPINGS ARE FROM 'WISE ACRES' PUBLICATIONS FROM 1914 - 1918.

---

"How to tell the flowers from the weeds: pull them up by the roots. If they are flowers that will be the last of 'em; if weeds only the beginning..."

—Smiles, *Wise Acres*, June, 1915

# Diamonds of the Decades (1911–1920)

### FRANCIS GARDINER FINLETTER '15 (D.1985)

The first student, one of three by Christmas—*"A handful more and by spring a fair-sized group."* As a student, Francis was associate editor for *Wise Acres*. She vividly recalled *"dynamiting holes to set trees under Mr. Doan's eagle eye."* Her first job was with Miss Elizabeth Leighton Lee. Later, she was one of the first women accepted into membership in the American Society of Landscape Architects and was active in the profession for 55 years.

### MARJORIE McCREIGHT TROTTER '16 (D.1981)

During WWI, Marjorie worked among the mountain people of Tennessee teaching home and school gardening for the Department of the Interior. She married Thomas W. Miller who owned and operated Colonial Boxwood Co. After his death, she moved to Camden, SC and met her second husband, owner of Evergreen Nurseries. She quoted: *"I remarried but I do not seem able to get away from my profession. No doubt until I close my eyes I will be planting shrubs and trees for I love my work."*

### DOROTHY AND KATHERINE CLOUD '16

Following their time at the school, the sisters opened their own Horticultural Consultancy in addition to writing several gardening books. In 1924, Katherine wrote a letter to the school; *"I am very pleased to have this opportunity to express my deep appreciation for what the school has done... The excellent instruction both in theory and in practice... gave us a splendid foundation. I take this opportunity to thank the founders of the school for their vision in establishing such an institution, and to the able instructors which we were privileged to have."*

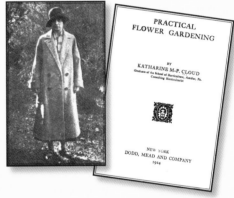

### JANE RIGHTER '17 & KATHARINE COHEN '17

While at PSHW, Katharine was involved in writing and publishing the school's newspaper, *Wise Acres*. During WWI, she worked with fellow graduate Jane Righter to help develop Victory Gardens. Jane was President of the Alumnae Association and later on the PSHW Board of Trustees. In 1941, the Greenwich, CT Garden Club endowed a Garden Club of America medal in her name. This prestigious medal is awarded to people who have outstanding achievements in rose culture.

**PHOTOGRAPHS:** "THE OLD BELL THAT CALLS TO MEALS" FROM THE SCHOOL PROSPECTUS, 1914; STUDENTS IN "MIDDY" SAILOR BLOUSES GIVE A GARDENING DEMONSTRATION IN THE NEW GREENHOUSE, 1914; KATHERINE CLOUD AS A STUDENT IN 1916; TITLE PAGE OF <u>PRACTICAL FLOWER GARDENING</u> ONE OF THE BOOKS WRITTEN BY THE CLOUD SISTERS; (LEFT) JANE RIGHTER AND KATHARINE COHEN ADVERTISE THEIR WORK IN COUNTRY LIFE MAGAZINE, 1917; STUDENTS PLANNING THE ROSE GARDEN NEAR THE BARN.

> "...objectives of the association were to promote interest and success in horticulture and agriculture by the exchange of information among its members."
> —*Wise Acres*, March, 1914.

The Blakiston family owned the farm adjacent to the school. In addition to financial support, the Blakiston women often gave lectures on a variety of topics and hosted tea parties for the students of PSHW.

From 1927 to 1934, Miss Emma Blakiston was chairperson for the Keystone division of the Woman's National Farm and Garden Association. In 2005, a group of women renewed Ambler's association with WNFGA and founded the Ambler Keystone Branch.

EMMA BLAKISTON
(1861-1942)

**AMBLER GAZETTE**
**THURSDAY, MAY 14, 1914**

**TO CONFER ON AGRICULTURE.**

WOMEN TO MEET AT AMBLER FARM SCHOOL MAY 16.

Wide Variety of Subjects Will Be Discussed by Experts from all Parts of the Country – Surprising Advances Made in Past Few Years.

**PHOTOGRAPHS:** (TOP LEFT) LOGO FOR THE WOMAN'S NATIONAL FARM & GARDEN ASSOCIATION; (TOP RIGHT) EMMA BLAKISTON, SUPPORTER OF PSHW AND WNFGA; (LEFT) ARTICLE FROM AMBLER GAZETTE, MAY 14, 1914, ANNOUNCING THE MEETING OF THE "NATIONAL ASSOCIATION OF WOMEN AGRICULTURISTS—ONE OF THE FIRST NAMES BY WHICH THE ASSOCIATION WAS KNOWN; (ABOVE) THE 2005 FOUNDING MEMBERS OF THE NEW AMBLER KEYSTONE WOMAN'S FARM & GARDEN BRANCH.

*Timeline...*

| MAY 17, 1913 | MAY 16, 1914 | MAY 18, 1916 | NOVEMBER, 1930 |
|---|---|---|---|
| A MEETING IS HELD IN THE BARN TO DISCUSS ORGANIZING A WOMEN'S AGRICULTURAL AND HORTICULTURAL ASSOCIATION. | FIRST CONFERENCE OF THE WOMEN'S NATIONAL AGRICULTURAL AND HORTICULTURAL ASSOCIATION IS HELD ON CAMPUS. | DURING THE SECOND ANNUAL MEETING, THE ORGANIZATION CHANGES ITS NAME TO "WOMAN'S NATIONAL FARM AND GARDEN ASSOCIATION." (WNFGA) | THE NEW EMBLEM, DESIGNED BY DR. HENRY TURNER BAILEY, IS UNVEILED AT THE 16TH ANNUAL MEETING HELD IN DETROIT. |

# CHAPTER 2: *Woman's National Farm and Garden Association*

In May of 1913, a Horticultural Conference was held in the barn at the School of Horticulture for Women. Over four hundred men and women attended. It was at this historic conference that the attendees voted to establish a National Women's Agricultural Association. At a consequent meeting in New York that same year, the Woman's National Agricultural and Horticultural Association came to fruition.

After the initial *"meeting in the barn"* a second meeting was called at the School of Horticulture the following year, and was declared a success with 450 attendees. During this meeting, the officers were elected and the Association became a reality. Ambler student, Miss Louise G. Davis, was appointed Treasurer of the new Association. Other Ambler members included Miss Jane Bowne Haines, Miss Elizabeth Leighton Lee, and Miss Emma Blakiston. The Founding President was Mrs. Francis King (Louisa) from Michigan.

**PHOTOGRAPH:** AN EARLY TOUR OF THE PENNSYLVANIA SCHOOL OF HORTICULTURE FOR WOMEN, PRIOR TO 1915 THE OLD FARMHOUSE WAS THE ONLY BUILDING THAT LINED THE ENTRANCE DRIVE.

As the first President of the Woman's National Farm & Garden Association, Mrs. Francis King led the Association for six years. She was also a noted author and published nine books in addition to numerous magazine articles. In her books, Mrs. King used her practical firsthand experience to explain garden design and horticulture to her mainly female readers. In one of her books, donated to the Ambler library by the WNFGA, Mrs. King wrote *"A garden! The end is in itself a picture, and what a picture it reveals!"*

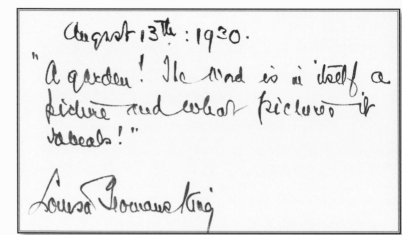

The call for members was sent out in March 1914, and membership dues were listed as $1.00 per year with an additional $1.00 joining fee. In its initial year, the Association drew 500 members from across the nation. With new names added daily, the women expected to draw over 1000 members before their next annual meeting. *"Everywhere the idea of a national organization to rouse interest in agriculture and horticulture among women is hailed with the greatest enthusiasm and all who attended the conference felt the progressive spirit manifest at the meeting," Wise Acres*, June, 1914.

By 1916, although the Association was solidified, the name remained transient. At the Annual Meeting held in Boston on May 16, 1916, a debate arose regarding the choice of name.  Mirroring their British counterparts, the women chose to change the words in their title from *"agricultural and horticultural"* to *"farm and garden."* However, in true American style, the women chose to honor the importance of the individual and used *"Woman's"* rather than the British "Women's," which recognized the collective effort. And thus they became the Woman's National Farm and Garden Association.

The women of PSHW remained dedicated members of the WNFGA and as one of the vice-presidents, Elizabeth Leighton Lee travelled across the nation to attend the various meetings and events held by the association. On October 2nd, 1916, she travelled to Chicago to attend a three day meeting of the Midwest branch. During the meeting, the shortage of farm labor was a main topic of discussion, and it was decided that a telegram would be sent to the President, Woodrow Wilson, asking him to mobilize all unemployed men for such labor. It was decisions such as these that emphasized the importance and necessity of the organization not only for the advancement of women, but for all associated with agriculture in the United States and abroad.

**PHOTOGRAPHS:** (TOP RIGHT) AN INSCRIPTION IN ONE OF MRS. KING'S GARDEN BOOKS; (ABOVE LEFT) FAITH TIBERIO WELCOMES CURRENT WNFGA PRESIDENT MARY BERTOLINI AND THE ASSOCIATION TO THE FUTURE WNFGA VISITOR CENTER AT AMBLER ARBORETUM; (ABOVE CENTER) WNFGA VISITING THE AMBLER ARBORETUM IN 2008; (ABOVE RIGHT) HAZEL HERRING SPEAKS WITH ARBORETUM DIRECTOR JENNY ROSE CAREY AS MARLA DIAMOND LOOKS ON.

The Ambler Keystone branch was founded after the Historic Marker Dedication and the 2005 Philadelphia Flower Show exhibit revealed the strong link between the Farm and Garden Association and the Ambler Campus. The first meeting of the new group was held in September 2005 in the old red barn, now the gymnasium, to echo the initial meetings here at Ambler in 1913 and 1914. Jenny Rose Carey was the founding president of the Ambler Keystone Branch. The Bucks County Branch was founded as a sister group in 2010 with Linda Cotilla as first president. The groups maintain strong connections. The Woman's National Farm and Garden Association has been a strong supporter of the Ambler campus and its programs. The individual branches and Divisions have supported many different scholarships and have given generously to support the new Visitor's Center and the Hilda Justice Artifacts Collection.

**PHOTOGRAPHS:** (TOP LEFT) 2009 AMBLER KEYSTONE BRANCH; (TOP RIGHT) FAITH TIBERIO; (ABOVE) GROUP PHOTO OF THE WNFGA MEMBERS AT AMBLER ARBORETUM DURING THEIR VISIT TO THE AMBLER ARBORETUM IN JUNE, 2008.

# WWI and the Women's Land Army

"The school was invited to march in the Second-Line-of-Defense Parade in Philadelphia on April 20th, 1918, and the invitation was accepted with great enthusiasm. Placards bearing slogans for each department were made by the students... The school costume of 'Duxbak' with a green sash and hoe over the shoulder was decided to be the appropriate marching costume—so the students dressed in this fashion, started out though the rain was falling and a cold east wind blowing."

—*Wise Acres,* July, 1918

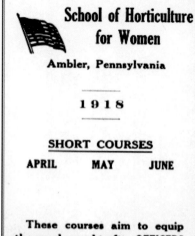

**PHOTOGRAPHS:** (LEFT) WOMEN'S LAND ARMY, (ABOVE) WWI CLIPPINGS: FROM WISE ACRES, MARCH, 1918; (BELOW) AN ADVERTISEMENT FROM THE 1925 VIEWBOOK SENT OUT TO PROSPECTIVE STUDENTS.

During the First World War, the United States Defense Council requested that the Woman's National Farm & Garden Association join other women's agricultural groups to form the "Women's Land Army of America." The school also added special war courses including "Captain's" and "Lieutenant's" courses and a canning kitchen to aid in the instruction of 20,000 "farmerettes" who plowed the land and provided food for thousands of soldiers and citizens in the United States and abroad. Students on campus were encouraged to volunteer extra hours in the gardens and canning kitchen to help maintain food rations. In the summer, they were paid twenty cents an hour and worked six hours a day, the same as other workers in the Women's Land Army of America.

### Ambler's Training Camp
PROMINENT WOMEN TAKE INTENSIVE WAR COURSES

During the actual war period, when Food Production and Preservation received such impetus, the School endeavored tirelessly to cope with all the demands made upon it.

It became a miniature training camp, with its army of women mobilized with hoe and rake. In referring to its usefulness, one prominent paper may be quoted as saying:—

"It seems almost providential that such a school should have been started just in time to be in full operation when the call for women labor has become imperative."—*Public Ledger.*

*Reproduced from photograph by Philadelphia Public Ledger, May 16, 1917*

After all was not tilling the soil while men of the family fought or hunted one of the oldest occupations of women?

Graduates were also involved in the war effort in victory gardens, work camps, and the Red Cross. As volunteers they were able to utilize the skills they had learned at PSHW.

One notable graduate, Emily David '16, was in charge of the victory gardens in Germantown and Chestnut Hill and director of a USO lounge.

# CHAPTER 3: *The Early Years—1920's*

Following World War I, an interest in horticulture and agriculture grew exponentially among women. In November of 1921, students could enroll for a January start and pay a yearly tuition of $200 for forty weeks, with an additional $475 for a single room and board. Summer courses were also offered at a rate of $25 per course with room and board provided for $12 to $14 per week.

By the 1920's, the uniform was altered once again and riding pants, or "jodhpurs," replaced the "Duxbak." These cropped pants extended to the knee and had an adjustable knee strap. The uniform was completed with a smock or shirtwaist, a soft brimmed hat, and "puttees," which were canvas leggings that reached from the top of the boot to the bottom of the pants.

The uniform was not the only thing that that changed in this decade. As the school's enrollment increased, so did the need for more student accommodation; and during the mid 1920's plans were laid out for a new dormitory. By 1928, ground was broken and construction on the building began. This new dormitory was to accommodate fifty students and would also have a dining hall, gathering room, classroom, recreational room, laundry room, and offices. Around the new dormitory, a new garden was to be laid out, replacing the vineyard and orchard. Each alumnae member gave a hemlock tree towards a hedge that would enclose the garden. Members of the Board also donated Japanese Cherry trees for planting two long aisles along the east and west sections of the garden. Meanwhile, the students began planting the perennial borders and the graduating class built a dry retaining wall for the terrace.

---

**SCHOOL OF COUNTRY LIFE**
Saturdays—April and May
at the
Pennsylvania School of Horticulture for Women
Ambler, Pennsylvania
Program 9:30 to 12:30
April 12—Dairy Day
April 19—Nature Study Day
April 26—Vegetable Garden Day
May 3—Bee Day and Poultry Day
May 10—Better Homes Day
May 17—Flower Garden Day
Specially adapted for Girl Scouts and High School Students who are interested in Nature Study and Country Life
Registration fee, ten cents. No tuition.
Train leaves Reading Terminal 8:02 A.M.

**PHOTOGRAPHS:** (TOP LEFT) A STUDENT WEARING DUXBAK EDGES THE GARDEN; (CENTER RIGHT) A STUDENT IN JODHPURS WORKS IN THE GREENHOUSE; (ABOVE LEFT) ADVERTISEMENT IN WISE ACRES, MARCH, 1924 FOR "SCHOOL OF COUNTRY LIFE" COURSES FOR YOUNG GIRLS; (ABOVE RIGHT) STUDENTS WORK IN THE DRAWING ROOM.

# Louise Carter Bush-Brown

In 1924, Louise Carter replaced Ms. Elizabeth Leighton Lee and took over the reins as director of the School of Horticulture for Women just eight years after graduating. During her years away from the school, she remained in contact with her Alma Mater, often writing to Wise Acres and even sending packages to former classmates. After her graduation in 1916, she took a position as a teacher at a school in Concord, Massachusetts. That year, she wrote *Wise Acres*: *"The location of the place is perfectly beautiful and the children are adorable, but I get pretty homesick for Ambler. I think of you so, so often."*

Louise had been editor of *Wise Acres*. As Director, she continued her writing, publishing several popular books, including the best selling, AMERICA'S GARDEN BOOK which she co-wrote with her husband, James Bush-Brown in 1939. In 1959, the revised edition was sent to the Brussels World Fair as one of America's top 10 books published that year.

During the Second World War, the school faced a serious crisis as students and faculty left to join the war effort, leaving no adequate replacements. Only a single man remained on campus and not even a boy could be found to mow the lawn, thus leaving Louise to teach almost all of the courses as well as milk the cows, tend to the chickens, and cultivate the gardens. Refusing to face catastrophe, Louise pulled the school through its seemingly insurmountable difficulties and was found *"mowing the lawn when the bells of peace proclaimed the end of the war,"* Pen & Trowel, Spring 1949.

In 1953, Louise started the Neighborhood Garden Association of Philadelphia, which aimed to increase self pride in homeowners and low income neighborhoods. In 1959, she received a National Recreational Award for the Neighborhood Garden Project. Later, in 1967, she also spoke at the White House for a conference on Natural Beauty and Citizen Participation regarding her work. In 1953, Louise Carter Bush-Brown resigned from her position with PSHW and in 1968 the Alumni Association created a scholarship for second year students in her name. Outside of PSHW, she was also recognized for her horticultural influence by other associations. In 1949, Louise received a Doctor of Letters from Beaver College (Arcadia). In 1966, she received the Gold Medal Award of Massachusetts Horticultural Society and a Citation by the American Horticultural Society. Most recently, the Formal Gardens of Ambler Arboretum were re-dedicated in her honor.

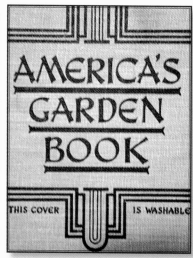

**PHOTOGRAPHS:** (TOP LEFT) MRS. LOUISE CARTER BUSH-BROWN AS FACULTY IN 1937; (ABOVE LEFT) FACULTY IN 1945; (ABOVE CENTER) COVER OF MR. AND MRS. BUSH-BROWN'S <u>AMERICA'S GARDEN BOOK</u>—NOTE THE ADVERTISEMENT "THIS COVER IS WASHABLE;" (ABOVE RIGHT) MR. AND MRS. BUSH-BROWN GREET THE FIRST RECIPIENT OF THE BUSH-BROWN SCHOLARSHIP, KENNETH YOUNG, IN 1969.

# The Apple Harvest

Since the early days of the School of Horticulture the apple orchard was always a valuable part of the school, not only for pruning and dynamite lessons, but also for the delicious apples which the students pressed into apple cider and sold at farmer's markets and Harvest Fairs. In preparation for the Fair, students picked the apples; sorting out the best ones for sale and making cider of the rest, under the direction of their fruit instructor. The annual apple harvest became one of those school traditions for which Jane Bowne Haines had aspired. Despite the hard work that went into the harvest, the sweet rewards are still fondly remembered by the alumni today.

Ken LeRoy '84 muses, *"I have made a career out of the skills learned in the orchard; growing a crop, plant healthcare, spraying, grafting, pruning and delighting in the harvest."*

**PHOTOGRAPHS:** (TOP LEFT) STUDENTS HARVESTING APPLES; (TOP RIGHT) STUDENTS WITH THE WORKHORSE AND FARM CART TAKING THE APPLES TO MARKET; (CENTER LEFT) STUDENTS WITH THE APPLE HARVEST READY FOR SALE; (CENTER RIGHT) STUDENTS PRUNING THE APPLE TREES; (ABOVE RIGHT) MALE STUDENTS PRESS THE APPLE CIDER IN THE 1960'S.

# Diamonds of the Decades (1920–1929)

## MARGARET ENGLAND '24 & RUBY C. PANNAL '24

"RICH NECK FARM", MD

They started with 1000 apple trees and a very successful herd of Jersey cows with excellent records and show string. Ruby quotes: *"Rich Neck is a beautiful farm on a high bluff overlooking the Sassafras River. The fertile field and shrubbery all attest to the good training we got at Ambler."*

## ELIZABETH C. HALL '24 (D. 1989, AGE 91)

As a student, Elizabeth packed cut flowers and fruit, kept bees, sold produce at the roadside stand, cleaned the chicken coops, and fired the dormitory's coal furnace; all to earn her tuition and board. She came to the school with a degree in Chemistry from Radcliffe College and Master's in Library Science from Columbia. She was librarian at the Horticultural Society of New York from 1930-37 and then librarian and assistant curator of the New York Botanical Gardens for twenty years. For these two positions she received the appellation Librarian and Assistant Curator of Education Emerita.

## ESTELLE L. SHARP '26

A lecturer, writer, and teacher, Estelle was also Director of the Philadelphia Horticultural Society (PHS) in 1952 and taught adult evening classes for PHS at Radnor High School. She also lectured on horticulture classes at a Philadelphia Judging School. She assisted with writing and editing THE WOMAN'S HOME COMPANION GARDEN BOOK.

## ANNE WERTSNER WOOD '27

*"Bold-lipped, rich tinted as the sea. The brown eyes radiant with vivacity. Anne can crowd more activities into twelve hours than a normal mortal can in twenty-four"* is the quote from her yearbook page.

She taught floriculture from 1929-36 and was PHS Field Secretary—leading tours and giving lectures. She staged the Philadelphia Flower Show for 10 years and wrote THE FLOWER SHOW GUIDE. She also wrote, MAKE YOUR OWN MERRY CHRISTMAS and provided a chapter on "Propagation" for Mrs. Sharp's book, as well as most of the Kodachrome illustrations. In 1969, she received a Certificate of Honor from Temple and in 1979, a Certificate of Merit from PHS that proclaimed: *"As a tree is known by its fruits, so is a teacher by her pupils."* She remained an avid gardener, propagating her favorite shrubs from home and planting new ones in her small garden when she moved into a retirement community.

**PHOTOGRAPHS:** (THIS PAGE) STUDENTS CULTIVATE THE VEGETABLE GARDEN. **OPPOSITE PAGE:** (TOP ROW L-R) "WOULD BE FARMERS" OF PSHW; MISS. HALL ARRIVES AT PSHW; "RUBY" PANNAL, "GINY" ENGLAND, "MAG" YOSKUM, "TOM" HALL; (BOTTOM ROW) MISS. HALL AND MRS. BUSH-BROWN TRANSPORTING COWS, NEWLY ARRIVED FROM GEORGIA; MISS TWINING, MISS HALL, AND MISS CLARK GUARD THE SIGNPOST; (RIGHT) MARTHA TWINING WITH HORSES AND PLOUGH IN 1924.

## MARTHA BRYANT '29 (D. 1967) & GISELLA GRIMM '29 (D. 1992)

"BRYGRIM FARMS," VA
"Mike" and "Gee" owned a successful landscaping business with a fine herd of Aberdeen Angus cattle and purebred Hampshire and Dorset sheep. For her work on the Audubon Weyanoke Sanctuary, Gisela received the National Audubon Society's William Dutcher Award and the Garden Club of Virginia's Meritorious Achievement Award.

## PAULINE LEIBERT STOCKER '29 (D.1985)

"Polly" was devoted to her Alma Mater and loyally served the alumni association in many ways. After graduation she served as Secretary of Bureau of Vocation, designed to track the whereabouts of the graduates and line up jobs for future graduates. She also ran the "Meats Booth" at the annual Harvest Fair, procuring delicious hams, bacon, and sausage the old Pennsylvania Dutch way. Professionally, Pauline designed and maintained many private gardens.

**STABLE & CORRAL**

**GREENHOUSES, COLDFRAMES & POTTING SHED**

**BARNS & SILO**

**ORIGINAL FARMHOUSE**

**WELLINGTON: THE DEAN'S COTTAGE**

**1929 DORMITORY**

**CHICKEN HOUSES**

**1915 DORMITORY & CLASSROOM**

28

*Timeline...*

### 1930

THE PERENNIAL BORDERS ARE ESTABLISHED AND THE GRADUATING CLASS BUILDS THE DRY RETAINING WALL.

### 1935

STUDENTS HOLD A DAIRY SHOW. DISPLAYING THE BEST OF THEIR PRIZE WINNING JERSEY DAIRY HERD, THEY TAKE HOME SEVERAL AWARDS.

### 1937

UPON THE DEATH OF FOUNDER JANE BOWNE HAINES, MRS. R. MARSHALL TRUITT TAKES OVER AS PRESIDENT OF THE BOARD OF DIRECTORS.

### 1938

TWO NEW GREENHOUSES ARE ADDED AND THE POTTING SHED IS BUILT.

# CHAPTER 4: *A Growing Campus—1930's*

In 1929, the new dormitory was completed. Upon entering the central reception area, a hallway to the left and the stairway led to student rooms. The hallway to the right, containing offices and an alumnae room, led to the dining room (west wing) and kitchen. There was a student lounge, kitchenette and a smoking room in the east wing. A classroom, laundry room, and rec room were in the basement. Lois Woodward Paul '30 recalled moving into the new dormitory: *"It was a rainy spring and the construction site was quite muddy. We used Jackson the farm horse and a cart to move our belongings. Miss Barber, the housemother, was quite alarmed we were not careful in keeping our new house clean."* By 1930, the girls had planted the perennial borders in the formal gardens leading to the dormitory.

In 1935, the school proudly displayed their prize winning herd of Jersey cows by hosting their first Dairy Show. The school had received two calves from a neighboring farmer in the 1920's, but it was not until the 1930's that their herd began to grow.

During her time as Director, Mrs. Bush-Brown had been repeatedly asked to suggest a good farm digest. Louise decided that she could take a selection of international agricultural literature, condense and republish the best articles into one digest; and thus the idea of the *Farmers Digest* was born. Although it required a huge effort, Mrs. Bush-Brown with the help of her assistant Miss Heick, produced a sample copy for the Board of Directors. Encouraged by Mrs. Bush-Brown, the students began their publication of the Farmers Digest in 1937, and sold it for a small profit. Within ten years, the publication reached subscribers as far afield as China, Africa and Australia, and brought in a modest income for the school.

## LOCAL SCHOOL PUBLISHES

### School of Hotriculture for Women at Ambler Prints "The Farmer's Digest"

"The Farmer's Digest," a magazine for those strictly associated with or engaged in agricultural work in its varying phases, has made its appearance in volume one and numbers one and is dated for the month of May, 1937. In appearance and size it is very similar to the very popular "Readers' Digest." It is to be published monthly at Ambler by the School of Horticulture.

From more than two hundred magazines and bulletins published in this country and abroad, the editorial staff of "The Farmer's Digest" selects articles of outstanding merit and general interest. It is comprehensive in its scope and covers all phases o agriculture. As far as is known, there is no other publication like it. The magazine sells for 25 cents the copy or $2.00 per year. Foreign subscription $3.00 per year.

The managing editor is L. Bush-Brown, and the assistant editors are John A. Andrew, C. Leavitt Dyer and Dr. R. L. Patrick. It is printed by the Johnson Press, Ambler, has a hundred pages and is chock full of meaty articles of interest to the agriculturist.

PHOTOGRAPHS: (TOP RIGHT ) ENTRANCE HALL OF DORMITORY; (CENTER) FARMERS DIGEST 1948; (ABOVE LEFT) CHERRY ALLÉES; (ABOVE RIGHT) STUDENTS WORKING IN THE PERENNIAL BORDER IN FRONT OF THE DORMITORY; (BOTTOM LEFT) STUDENTS TENDING THE HOLLYHOCKS; (BOTTOM CENTER) A STUDENT FEEDS THE JERSEY HEIFERS; (BOTTOM RIGHT) CLIPPING FROM THE AMBLER GAZETTE, MAY 6, 1937.

James Bush-Brown, husband of Louise Bush-Brown, laid out the original plan of the gardens around the new dormitory upon its completion. He was a landscape architect and an instructor of landscape design. Beatrix Farrand, friend of the school, and the only female founding member of the American Society of Landscape Architects, designed the pavilions which were later dedicated to Jane Linn Bright.

A statue of a young girl emptying her bucket into the pool was later added to the pavilions and students instantly declared it to be the new meeting place, often making plans to meet by the *'kid with the pitcher.'*

PHOTOGRAPHS: (TOP) THE FORMAL GARDENS, 1941; (CENTER LEFT) MR. BUSH-BROWN; (ABOVE LEFT) VESPERS BY THE FOUNTAIN, 1952; (LOWER RIGHT) VIEW OF THE DORMITORY FROM THE PAVILION, 1945.

Today, the Louise Bush-Brown Formal Gardens are the centerpiece of the Ambler Arboretum used for teaching, graduations and parties. Originally laid out on axis with the stone dormitory; the bi-laterally symmetrical gardens have been tended by students and staff since the 1920's. Old photographs show the women of PSHW in jodhpurs next to spires of delphinium and hollyhocks. The charm of the intensely planted mixed borders is still retained to this day allowing visitors to appreciate the carefully landscaped and nationally acclaimed Formal Gardens.

PHOTOGRAPHS: (TOP) A GARDENER TRIMS THE HEDGES IN THE FORMAL GARDENS, 2011; (ABOVE LEFT) THE FORMAL GARDENS IN FALL, 2010; (ABOVE RIGHT) VIEW OF DIXON HALL FROM THE FORMAL GARDENS, 2011.

Among our students we have had graduates of the following Schools and Colleges:

### PREPARATORY SCHOOLS

| | |
|---|---|
| The Agnes Irwin School | Kent Place School |
| The Baldwin School | The Mary A. Burnham School |
| Berkeley Institute | Mlle. Rey's School, Paris |
| Birmingham School | The Madiera School |
| Bradford Academy | National Cathedral School |
| The Brearley School | Oldfields |
| The Chapin School | Ogontz School |
| Chatham Hall | Penn Hall |
| Dana Hall | Sea Pines |
| Ecole Brillantmont | Stuart Hall |
| Friends' School, New York | The Spence School |
| Friends' Central School | The Shipley School |
| Friends' Select School | St. Agnes, Albany |
| The Gateway | St. Mary's Hall |
| George School | St. Mary's, Peekskill |
| The Holman School | Miss Wright's School |
| Horace Mann School | York Collegiate Seminary |

### COLLEGES

| | |
|---|---|
| Bryn Mawr | Vassar |
| Goucher | Wellesley |
| Hood | Wells |
| Mount Holyoke | Westhampton College |
| N. J. College for Women | Wheaton |
| Radcliffe | Western Reserve |
| Smith | Wilson |
| Swarthmore | University of Michigan |
| Sweet Briar | |

Positions held by graduates of the School of Horticulture:

Instructor in Gardening at Carson College.
Horticultural Therapist in a Hospital for Mental Diseases.
Librarian for the New York Horticultural Society.
Assistant in the Editorial Dept. of a Horticultural Pub. Co.
Farm Manager at an Industrial School for Girls.
Poultry Superintendent at an Industrial School for Girls.
Garden Consultants.
Superintendent of a Commercial Nursery.
Manager of the Display Gardens of a large Nursery.
Garden Agents under the Government Extension Service.
Superintendents of Private Estates.
Teachers of Gardening at Settlement Houses.
Supervisor of the Retail Dept. of a Commercial Nursery.
Garden Director at The Fellowship Center.

### LOIS WOODWARD PAUL '30 (D.1985)

Lois returned to Ambler to teach and head the Floriculture Department after receiving a graduate degree from Smith College. From 1956-60 she was a Field Lecturer for PHS and also served on the Executive Council. She later joined Longwood Gardens in 1960 as Director of the Department of Education. Lois received the Distinguished Achievement Award of PHS- the highest award given. In 1968 she received the Temple University Certificate of Honor.

### IDELLA KRAUSE '30 (D.1973)

After a succesful career in business, she came to Ambler to study poultry, but later recognized her skills in the world of horticulture. With her partner Rena Middleton, she designed and landscaped the Bird House in the Philadelphia Zoo in 1949. She also designed and supervised a new rose garden at the Zoo. For 21 years, she served as Treasurer of the Alumni Association and was always active in the Harvest Fairs.

### MARTHA LUDES GARRA '30 (D.1998)

Better known as "Janie." In the 1940's, Martha was Eastern Regional Chairman of the sub-committee on food conservation of the Victory Garden Committee. She designed the Physic Garden at the Pennsylvania Hospital. In the Fall of 1947, she gave a series of floriculture lectures at the School of Horticulture. Martha also served as the Executive Secretary for the Alumni Association and was elected to the school's Board of Directors in 1949.

### MARY PIERCY LOTT '31 (D.1969)

Mary's family owns and operates Bear Mountain Orchards in Aspers, PA near Gettysburg. The farm has over 500 acres of mostly fruit trees—sweet and sour cherries, plums, prunes, peaches, apples, and pears. In season, sweet corn is raised and marketed. The farm has a packing shed for packing, selling and shipping the fruit. The family was devoted to agriculture—through 4-H clubs and committee work on water and soil conservation.

## ELYONTA HARSHBERGER '32 (D.1990)

Elyonta was a registered landscape architect in PA and NY after she received her degree from University of Pennsylvania. She lived in Abington where she did design work on residential properties, office buildings, factories, schools, restoration, and low cost housing units. In 1962, she was the landscape architect for the South Jersey Colonial Village, built around the Smithville Inn, an old stagecoach inn, near Atlantic City.

## DR. ELIZABETH CLARK '35

For 7 years she was a staff member of the Brooklyn Botanical Garden and gave short courses on plants and trees. During WWII she gave lectures on Victory Gardens. In 1948 she moved to Baltimore and was Supervisor of Gardens and Nature Activities for the Baltimore Bureau of Recreation. Elizabeth was one of the originators of Cylburn Wildflower Preserve and Garden Center, which later became the first arboretum in Maryland.

## MARION BLACK WILLIAMS '37 (D.1975)

A writer and editor, during WWII, Marion wrote a daily column on victory gardens. She also edited and contributed to High Altitude Gardening and was later editor of MOUNTAIN AREAS, FLOWER AND GARDEN MAGAZINE. In New Mexico, she was the founder and President of Los Alamos Garden Club. In 1953, she went to Colorado and taught several gardening courses at the UCO, and was also a founding member of the Horticultural Arts Society.

## MARY ENCK REITER '39

Mary's home was a farm in Biglerville, PA where she raised a dairy herd, field crops, and vegetables. After her graduation, Mary returned to PSHW to teach riding and poultry. She also worked on the Farmer's Digest with Miss Heick. Mary quotes *"I have special feelings for Ambler. I worked there 4 years after graduation and ...later we lived in part of the old farm house (Haines House) nearest the road for 3 years... It was like my second home."*

**PHOTOGRAPHS:** CLASS OF 1937 POSES IN FRONT OF THE OLD SCHOOL BUILDING, NOW THE ADMINISTRATION BUILDING.
**OPPOSITE PAGE:** (TOP) 1935-6 VIEWBOOK PAGE 3, DETAILING WHERE STUDENTS CAME FROM AND WHERE THEY WENT AFTER PSHW; (BOTTOM) 1939 CLASS 50TH ANNIVERSARY REUNION.

On the home front, along with the production and preservation of vegetables, dairy was an important part of the Second Line of Defense in World War II. In 1940, the school's Jersey cattle herd was highly recognized and won a gold medal for being the highest producing dairy herd in Pennsylvania. Elsewhere, with the majority of men commissioned in the Armed Forces, many women either personally went to help dairy farmers who were short-handed, or they assisted with work placements for students. One graduate, Nannie Humphreys '43 owned a family homestead of 130 acres where she wrote *"government projects take all my laborers... working alone, pastures, hogs, poultry, and sheep... cannot always sleep so I knit for the Red Cross."* She was over 60 years old at the time.

**PHOTOGRAPHS:** AGRICULTURAL STUDENTS HERDING THE SCHOOL'S CATTLE. **OPPOSITE PAGE:** (TOP RIGHT) STUDENTS BRINGING IN THE HARVEST, 1943; (BOTTOM) STUDENTS WORKING IN THE VEGETABLE GARDEN—DURING WWII, STUDENTS WERE ABLE TO UTILIZE THEIR TRAINING FROM PSHW TO GROW THOUSANDS OF SEEDLINGS FOR THE VICTORY GARDENS THEY SUPERVISED.

34

*Timeline...*

**SEPTEMBER 1, 1939**

BEGINNING OF WWII. GRADUATES ARE PLACED IN POSITIONS OF GREAT RESPONSIBILITY, OFTEN TAKING THE PLACE OF MEN WHO ARE FIGHTING THE WAR.

**1940**

STUDENTS ARE INVOLVED ON THE HOME FRONT - JOINING THE RED CROSS, VICTORY GARDENS, VOLUNTEERING AT BASES, AND JOINING WOMEN'S UNITS.

**1941**

ONLY ONE MAN LEFT ON CAMPUS - THE FARMER. THERE IS NO COOK, NO JANITOR, AND NO SECRETARY. MANY STAFF LEAVE FOR BETTER PAID POSITIONS WITH THE ARMED FORCES.

**1946**

SCHOOL OF HORTICULTURE APPROVED FOR VETERAN'S EDUCATION.

# CHAPTER 5: *The War Years—1940's*

## *Women who Served*

As the United States once again entered war, the Pennsylvania School of Horticulture did its part in the war effort. A summer program was initiated with special emphasis on food production and preservation by canning. Many students joined the war effort supervising victory gardens or taking positions with the Red Cross, Women's Land Army, and later with the Women's Army Corps (WAC), Women's Coast Guard (SPAR—*Semper Parátus*), and Women's Army Service Pilots (WASPs).

A large number of graduates from the 1930's were involved in the war effort overseas, working in Japan, China, Korea, the Philippines, Australia, Canada, Great Britain, France, Dutch New Guinea, New Guinea, and regions in Africa. Joan Hogg '29 travelled to Australia to assist with the 1600 member Women's Land Army of Australia. Also in Australia, Jane Kenworthy '36 worked as a Red Cross Commander. In 1943, she wrote to *Pen & Trowel* that she was *"with Club Mobile Unit—driver, mechanic, cook, entertainer, gypsy."*

Graduates of the School of Horticulture also worked in counter-intelligence. For 25 years, Ellen Tilden Milligen '35 worked with the CIA in various positions across Asia. In Africa, Betty Van Sant McDonald '40 did classified map work for the Army Map Service under the guise of Soil Conservation Bureau. Another graduate, Fleda Ochsner '37, completed secret war work for Polaroid Company in Okinawa, Japan. Other students also travelled to Japan, where they worked with the Red Cross and WAC. While in Japan, 1943 graduate Francesca Brickhead was able to visit fellow graduate Michi Yamaguchi, who had studied at the School of Horticulture in 1942 and later returned to Japan in the midst of the war to start a horticultural school there.

In 1944, Mary Green '38 was in charge of an experimental garden project to be used as a part of the psychiatric treatment for "war neurosis" cases at the Swarthmore annex of the Philadelphia Naval Hospital. She continued working in horticulture therapy for "combat fatigue" of Marines returning from the Pacific in 1945. In 1949, Mary wrote to *Pen & Trowel* that she *"has forsaken horticulture for the duration and is doing Chemical War work in South Philadelphia."*

No matter their position on the home front or overseas, students and graduates of the School were encouraged by their education. As the father of 1939 graduate, Mary Louise Beardsley wrote: *"She had little thought that when she attended the School of Horticulture that her training there would prove of the greatest benefit to her in her life in war time England."*

> **"If there is one lesson in history that is unmistakable it is that national strength lies very near the soil."**
> —Daniel Webster

**PHOTOGRAPHS:** (TOP) MR. BUSH-BROWN TEACHES LANDSCAPE DESIGN ON THE TOP FLOOR OF THE 1915 DORMITORY; (LOWER LEFT) STUDENTS DRAFT BLUEPRINTS FOR LANDSCAPE DESIGN; (LOWER RIGHT) STUDENTS CONCENTRATE DURING A BOTANY CLASS.

*Timeline...*

### 1940

THE ADJACENT BLAKISTON FARM IS PURCHASED, ADDING 116 ACRES TO THE SCHOOL CAMPUS. DR. RUTH PATRICK, BOTANY TEACHER 1940-45

### 1941

A WORK-STUDY PROGRAM IS OFFERED. IN 1947, MRS. EDWARD C. LUKENS IS HIRED TO DIRECT THE SUMMER CAMPS.

### 1947

SCHOOL OPENED AT CAPACITY - 55 STUDENTS RESIDENT IN THE DORM, 6 IN THE COTTAGE, AND SEVERAL OLDER STUDENTS LODGED NEARBY.

### 1946

CHANGE IN ALUMNAE BY-LAWS; HALF OF DUES NOW GO TOWARDS AN ALUMNAE GIFT TO THE SCHOOL TO BE USED FOR SOMETHING ESPECIALLY NEEDED.

# The Industrious Forties

During the war years the school continued to expand as women took a strong interest in farm and agricultural courses to help feed the nation. At the conclusion of the war, women continued to flock to the school, and in 1947, the school opened at capacity. Contrasting with the interest in farm and agriculture courses that proved popular during the war, new students showed a stronger interest in horticulture and landscape design. In 1946, there were 27 students enrolled in these courses—nearly half of the student population. To accommodate this growing interest, the school added a new greenhouse for work in experimental botany, a new rose garden and a delphinium trial garden.

The uniform of the 1940's reflected the societal changes that had occurred during the war. Out were the days of skirts and blouses, now the women were permitted to wear plain tailored shirts, culottes and riding breeches/jodhpurs. In winter it was suggested that the women wear ski pants and green or brown jackets. Sweaters and jeans, designed for wear by girls, were also permitted. In later years, blue jeans were reserved for outdoor work in the fields and greenhouses.

In the 1940's the school's Farmers Digest achieved great success as publication rose from 50 to 8,000 copies sold. In turn, the profit gained was used towards various projects on campus. In 1942, students used $365 of the profit to paint the barn. In 1943, $1200 paid for the construction of the stables and in the following year, they were able to purchase a new tractor. In 1945, the graduating class donated a structure to house the old farm bell conveniently situating it on the lawn midway between the dining hall and the kitchen.

In addition to calling the women in from the fields for dinner, the bell would ring every morning when classes ended at 10:10, to announce the *"milk break."* Eagerly the students would head for the *"stage area of the dining room"* where the cart of milk and home-baked cookies or breads awaited. After a brief twenty minute respite, the women, now revived, would return to their classes.

In 1949, several more structures were added to the campus. The most notable was the large dairy barn which would accommodate 28 cows. Laurie Eaton, the daughter of the former agricultural instructor Mary Enck Reiter '39, recalls observing the students as a young girl; *"I was allowed to enter the barn where I sat and watched as the students milked the cows. I was just fascinated by them."*

### PRUNING THE APPLE TREES

Mrs. Louise Clark Flyger '41 remembers the cold winters when *"Dr. Andrews stayed inside and stayed warm while we were out in the cold pruning the apple trees—this is a famous memory!"*

**PHOTOGRAPHS:** (TOP RIGHT) STUDENT ON NEW TRACTOR, 1944; (CENTER LEFT) DEDICATION OF THE NEW BELL STRUCTURE, 1945; (BOTTOM LEFT) REITER FAMILY; BOB AND MARY WITH THEIR CHILDREN, ROBERT AND LAURIE—THE CHILDREN ARE DRESSED TO PARTICIPATE IN THE 1950 MAY DAY FESTIVITIES; (BOTTOM CENTER) THE OLD DAIRY BARN; (BOTTOM RIGHT) DOROTHY "DUTCH" AMMERMAN '43 PRUNES AN APPLE TREE.

# Agriculture at Ambler

Like the school itself, the agricultural program at the School of Horticulture had a modest start. Initially, the only agricultural courses offered were poultry and beekeeping, both of which were specifically selected due to their profit raising potential. The school's flock of egglayers consisted mainly of Single Comb White Leghorn chickens, but also included Plymouth Rocks, Rhode Island Reds, White Wyandottes, and Light Brahmas, most of which were only for educational purposes. In 1925, with the assistance of the chicken farmer, Mr. Cobleigh, the school reared around 1000 chicks, giving the school a nearly full sized commercial model. Less than five years later, the school expanded its entire agricultural program to include sheep, goats, pigs, and cattle. The agricultural program was very popular for the duration of its existence as women sought a higher education and enjoyed the hands on experience incorporated with the classroom learning. Although an "Aggie's" work was not easy, their country life was well enjoyed.

## A TYPICAL DAY FOR AN "AGGIE"

**Early morning (6 or 6:30AM)**
*Awake and ready to work!:*

SMALL ANIMALS *(poultry, sheep, pigs)*: Feed and water animals; collect eggs.

STABLES: Muck the stalls; give water, hay, and grain; groom the horses.

DAIRY: Set up milkers, feed calves, heifers, and cows; milk; pasteurize the milk; when finished, clean up the milking equipment. Student's were also responsible for keeping the dairy barn and heifer barn clean and neat.

**Midday (12–1PM):**

SMALL ANIMALS: Repeat AM duties as needed.

STABLES: Water and hay to the horses; muck the stalls.

DAIRY: Water and hay to calves and heifers; cows in pasture.

**Evening (4:30PM):**

*Repeat of morning duties after classes finished, then shower and change. All students had to wear dresses or skirts to the dining room for the evening meal, no slacks or shorts were allowed, and definitely no work boots!*

Over the decades, the students at PSHW participated in and organized many local and national agricultural shows and state fairs. In the early years, the women preened their chickens, occasionally coloring them blue and manicuring their beaks and claws with orangewood sticks before showing them. With the introduction of the dairy herd and the construction of stables for the horses, students later participated in dairy and horse shows.

Dairy shows were organized and presented usually in April by the Dairy Club. Any student could join, but usually it was the "Aggies". Each student was assigned a cow or heifer to train and get fit for show. Animals had to be trained to lead and stand properly. Animals were also judged on the cleanliness and suppleness of their coat, polish of their horns and hooves, clean ears, and a clean and fluffy tail. This was obtained by braiding the tail when wet, allowing it to dry overnight; then combing it out, in an upside-down manner so it fluffed. When participating in a show, students wore dress whites in the 4-H show model.

Horse shows were both a show of horsemanship and gymkhana with privately owned horses shown by their owners or guest riders (other students) if the owner approved. School horses were shared by lot for the various classes by the other students. The first recorded show on campus was in the spring of 1957, with nine classes; including 3-gait horsemanship, pleasure, jumping, novice, and bareback, and musical chairs for fun. All eight of the school's horses performed in the show. Horses owned by students Anne Clifford, Lenore Fried, Helene Zimmerman, Rita Pfaffinger, and Mary Anne Blair also competed. Subsequent shows became much more formal and the competition was stiffer. These later shows began at 8 am and lasted all day. As the school outgrew its simple country beginnings, the agricultural program came to an end.

**PHOTOGRAPHS:** (LEFT) THE 1958 DAIRY CLUB PREPARES FOR A CAMPUS FITTING AND SHOWMANSHIP DAIRY SHOW WITH PRESIDENT MARY ANNE FRY HOLDING THE HEAD OF CHIFFON THE COW; (ABOVE RIGHT) A STUDENT IN THE 1950'S POSES ON HER HORSE; (RIGHT) A PARTICIPANT IN A LOCAL HORSE SHOW IN 1937. **OPPOSITE PAGE:** (TOP ROW L-R) MARIAN AMMAN WITH TERRIBLE TENDER THE LAMB (ONE OF MANY ANIMALS RAISED IN THE DORMITORY!); SEVERAL OF THE SCHOOL'S PUREBRED SHEEP HERD; A STUDENT FEEDS ONE OF THE SCHOOL'S PIGS; (LOWER ROW L-R) AN "AGGIE" FEEDS THE CHICKENS; AGRICULTURAL STUDENTS LEAD THE COWS OUT OF THE BARN IN 1952; (INSET) PART OF A POEM FROM 'WISE ACRES' 1925

# May Day

May Day was the annual "Spring Fling." A time for merriment and joy; a time to invite family and friends to the school's frivolity; a time to enjoy the spring gardens. A May Queen, a senior, and her court were selected by vote of all of the students. The crowning of the Queen occurred and she was then entertained by her loyal subjects with drama and song in the 'garden theatre,' a dance around the May Pole and a display of prize winning animals. All were then invited to the "castle" (dormitory) for refreshments.

Ye are invited to
**MAY DAY**
at Ye
School of Horticulture
Sunday May 14, 1950.
2:30 P.M.
If Rain: May 21st

HERALD
Marie Clair Blumer
JUNIOR COURT
Lois Wenner            Marcia Lindsey
Georgia Johnson        Charlotte Gruber
Lois Nickerson         Marilyn Sulzbach
SENIOR COURT
Joan Kelly             Virginia Beekman
Helen Foster           Margaret Tyler
Daphne Ward            Grace Iseminger
FLOWER GIRL            Remona Deans
MAID OF HONOR
Betsy Booker
FLOWER GIRL            RING BEARER
Laurie Reiter          Stevie Petronsky
THE MAY QUEEN
Lee Sayre
Court Jester           Nancy Fostle

CROWNING OF THE MAY QUEEN

**PHOTOGRAPHS:** (TOP L-R) A 1950 MAY DAY INVITATION, COURTESY OF LOIS NICKERSON; MAY POLE DANCE; (2ND ROW L-R) HOPE GANDY LABARGE DRESSED UP ON HORSEBACK FOR THE 1957 MAY DAY PARADE; MARY ANNE FRY DRESSED UP AS THE JESTER WITH A PIGLET ON HARNESS FOR THE MAY DAY PLAY, 1957; (BOTTOM ROW L-R) THE MAY DAY PROGRAM, 1950; THE MAY DAY COURT, 1950.

# Nosen—Birth of our Sister School

On a fall day in 1940, a courageous young lady from Japan arrived to begin her studies in Horticulture at PSHW. Michi Yamaguchi came with best wishes from her sponsor Miss Michi Kawai; a Christian leader and internationally known educator. Miss Kawai had founded a school to train young women for work. After Michi Yamaguchi graduated, PSHW '42, she returned to Japan to direct the Horticultural and Agricultural programs at Nosen, using funds collected during the war. The school was on a rented site with *"dilapidated barracks—no heat, no glass in the windows, the only water supply a nearby stream."*

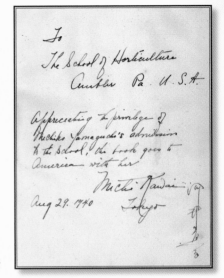

In 1952, Michi Yamaguchi wrote in Pen & Trowel; *"I am very glad that I went to the School of Horticulture... Living two years surrounded by the gardens, orchards and fields led me closer to nature. Carrying on lectures and practical work side by side gave me clearer understanding and deeper interest. The responsibility of duties was a good chance for me to approach the studies positively. The good given to me was so great that I am afraid I can't cover the whole or even realize the very core."*

After the death of Miss Kawai in 1953, Michi Yamaguchi assumed full responsibility of Nosen, along with another Ambler graduate, Setsu Inoue '54, who served as Michi's able assistant. Setsu spent three years in America; two at Ambler, a summer working at AmChem and a year more of study at Cornell. Setsu taught herbaceous plants, flower arranging, and landscape design.

The Japanese graduates of Ambler took many of the PSHW traditions back home with them: May Day celebration, with May Pole Dance and the crowning of a May Queen; correspondence with a little sister/pen pal; and at Christmas, the Peanut exchange. In 1946 the Ambler students sent a Christmas package to the Nosen students. A letter from Michi expressed their delight, *"When each package in the box was opened the cheers and cries of joy arose among them. We were so excited that we almost forgot the cold of the day; a moment before we were shivering."*

Setsu visited the Ambler campus in 1981; she came to America to study western floral design technique. Her oldest son, Hideto, also studied American floral design and assists his mother in the school flower shop.

Michi Yamaguchi retired as Director in 1981, but continued to teach at Nosen. Two more Ambler graduates have also taken their place on the Nosen teaching staff: Tsuneko Suzuki '59 and Asako Azuma '79.

**PHOTOGRAPHS:** (TOP LEFT) MICHI YAMAGUCHI; (TOP RIGHT) AN INSCRIPTION IN THE FRONT COVER OF MICHI KWAI'S BOOK THANKING THE SCHOOL FOR ACCEPTING MICHI YAMAGUCHI AS A STUDENT; (BOTTOM LEFT) A LITTLE SISTER/PEN PAL LETTER FROM KATSUKO TO LOIS NICKERSON; (BOTTOM CENTER) SETSU AT PSHW; (BOTTOM RIGHT) TSUNEKO "SUE" SUZUKI '59.

# Diamonds of the Decades (1940–1949)

### MARJORIE JOHNSON DIETZ '40

Marjorie is a writer and editor. She revised many books including: Roy Biles THE COMPLETE BOOK OF GARDEN MAGIC, the textbook used for Horticulture 15; and Rockwell & Grayson's THE COMPLETE BOOK OF BULBS used in Floriculture. Marjorie authored THE CONCISE ENCYCLOPEDIA OF FAVORITE FLOWERS AND THE CONCISE ENCYCLOPEDIA OF FAVORITE FLOWERING SHRUBS and several others. She was also an editor of Flower Grower magazine.

### JEAN BUTZ STONEBECK '41

A multi-talented woman, Jean is an entertainer, a speaker, a storyteller and a writer of fifteen books.

Due to her talents in story telling, she was known as "Aunt Lillie, the Story Lady." Jean also was employed as an historic tour guide and worked at the Lock Ridge Furnace Museum in Alburtis, PA. While there, she was instrumental in the restoration of a 19th century Iron Furnace, which was previously owned by the Butz family.

### LILLIAN LUBIN KRELOVE '41

Lillian worked at the school greenhouses for several of the spring plant sales where she enjoyed her connection to the students. She was also a writer and historian and wrote articles for Flower Grower Magazine after having been editor of the alumni newsletter Pen & Trowel for many years. After graduating from PSHW, Lillian remained active in alumni affairs at the campus.

### DR. RUTH YATES SCHMITZ '41

After her graduation, Ruth attended Wheaton College in Massachusetts where she worked as the Gardens, Trees and Shrubs Technician and maintained the campus grounds and greenhouse. She received her Ph.D in plant physiology from University of Wisconsin and later taught botany and plant physiology there. Ruth also grew thousands of vegetable seedlings for victory garden projects.

### JUNE VAIL '42

June was a lecturer and holly propagator. She was also considered an expert on South Jersey Pine Barrens where she led tours. June was always at the PHS information booth at the Flower Show and at PSHW Harvest Fairs with her native grasses and cones. She also assisted Mrs. Bush-Brown working with the Philadelphia 4-H clubs.

### EDNA PENNELL '43

After her studies at PSHW, Edna became a recognized authority for 18th century flower arrangements. She was employed as the Flower Arrangement Supervisor of Colonial Williamsburg for many years.

**OPPOSITE PAGE:** (TOP) TILLIE SPRAYS THE APPLE ORCHARD, 1942; (LEFT) AN ARTICLE ON LEONIE HAGERTY BELL; (CENTER) LEONIE'S YEARBOOK SELF PORTRAIT; (RIGHT) ONE OF LEONIE'S BOTANICAL DRAWINGS; (FAR RIGHT TOP) A 1946 BEEKEEPING CLASS; (FAR RIGHT BOTTOM) MYRT, PEARSALL, CREASY, CHICK, DUTCH, AND FRICK TAKING A BREAK IN THE WHEELBARROWS BY THE GREENHOUSE, 1942.

## LEONIE HAGERTY BELL '44
### (D.1996)

As an expert on old fashioned roses, and a self-employed botanical illustrator, Leonie wrote a book, THE FRAGRANT YEAR, which took 11 years to write while raising a family of 7. In 1945, with restrictions on printing due to the war, Leonie hand-sketched a yearbook for her entire graduating class. Later, she was able to use both her botanical knowledge and artistic skill to illustrate many books. She also wrote articles for *American Rose Annual*, and PHS Green Scene. In 1986, she received the Silver Honor Medal from the American Rose Society. Her work is currently represented in the drawing and print collection of the Hunt Botanical Library in Los Angeles.

**SELF-TAUGHT** . . . Leonie Bell, artist, author and lecturer, was acclaimed recently at the Hunt Botanical Library, Carnegie-Mellon University, Pittsburgh, where four of her botanical drawings were selected for inclusion in the second International Exhibition of Botanical Art. Mrs. Bell is a self-taught artist, having received no formal art training.

## CAROLYN COREY JARIN '46

Carolyn was founder and director of Peace Valley Nature Center in Bucks County, PA, for which she won numerous awards. She quoted; *"I kind of look at it, and all the success I've had with the nature center, as the right time and right place. I was lucky to be able to start this nature center because I had the horticulture and landscape background needed to do it."* In 1946, Carolyn wrote to Pen & Trowel that she had been looking for a farm in Bucks County. The salesman, Barney Jarin, eventually decided to show her his own farm in Chalfont. He quoted; *"It required no selling at all, Carolyn wanted a farm, and I wanted a wife."*

**PHOTOGRAPHS:** (TOP) 1952 AGRICULTURE STUDENTS "AGGIES" POSE ON THE HAY WAGON AS IT LEAVES THE BARN; (BOTTOM ROW L-R) STUDENTS TENDING THE FORMAL GARDENS; MRS. BUSH-BROWN AND MISS ANNA HEICK; RITA WIDMER MANAGES A STALL AT THE 1953 HARVEST FAIR; STUDENTS TRIMMING A HEDGE.

*Timeline...*

### 1951

MRS. LUKENS AND MR. PATRONSKY RUN A SUMMER FARM & GARDEN CAMP FOR 30 GIRLS AGED 13-18. THE RIDING PROGRAM IS VERY SUCCESSFUL.

### 1951

THE "NEW LIBRARY" IS COMPLETED. THE STONE FIREPLACE IS BUILT USING PROFITS FROM THE ALUMNAE ASSOCIATION HARVEST FAIR. THE RARE BOOK COLLECTION CONTAINS 200 VOLUMES.

### 1953

MRS. BUSH-BROWN RETIRES AND HER ASSISTANT MISS HEICK RETIRES IN 1954. MR. JONATHAN W. FRENCH, JR. IS APPOINTED DIRECTOR.

### 1955

THE FIRST DAUGHTER OF A GRADUATE ATTENDS— MOLLY JACKSON '57 DAUGHTER OF BERTHA LUBECK JACKSON '32.

# CHAPTER 6: *Transitional Times—1950's*

Leaving behind the struggle of the war years and the lack of staff to run the school, a brighter future was sought and the need to become an accredited school was apparent as more students wished to go on to further education. Students sought higher degrees in horticulture and related sciences, and the granting of an Associate of Science degree greatly enhanced the acceptance of their credits upon transfer.

In March of 1952, the school was admitted as a provisional member of the American Association of Junior Colleges, with five years of work for complete accreditation. The faculty was strengthened and English/Journalism and Social Studies were added to the curriculum. Dr. David Segal headed the Agriculture Department, Mr. Stephen Patronsky in Horticulture, with fruits and vegetables, Mr. J. Hapgood Brooks III, in Floriculture, and Mr. James Bush-Brown continued to teach Landscape Design. A required six week summer session was re-instituted to enhance the practical experience of the program. In 1954, the school was accepted conditionally into the Pennsylvania Association of Junior Colleges, another milestone attained. Four years later, the PA State Council gave permission for the school to change its name and grant the Associate of Science Degree. After much careful deliberation by the Board of Trustees the name "Ambler Junior College—A School of Horticulture for Women" was selected.

With their enhanced education, the young women were also expected to maintain proper composure and dining etiquette. Each incoming student was given a list of Dining Room Rules three pages long, which stated; *"Our relatively casual life in the country is no excuse for carelessness."* Some of the rules included; *"Avoid conversation from one table to another. Never cut up your entire serving of meat at one time. Fried chicken may be eaten with the fingers at a picnic, at the table use your knife and fork. Do not dip your own knife, fork or spoon into a sugar, jelly, relish or butter dish. Do not crumple your napkin in your glass."*

STUDENTS ENJOY A MEAL
IN THE DINING ROOM

## MRS. FRENCH'S BROWNIES

Nancy Reynolds Gibbons '58 fondly remembers the tea parties hosted by Mrs. French who would invite *"twenty or so ladies for tea in her home at Haines House on a Sunday afternoon. We would all be dressed up with our pocketbooks, which we had emptied of everything so that there would be plenty of room to bring back extra of Mrs. French's delicious brownies. She must have made hundreds of brownies even though there were never more than twenty girls at a time."*

## NEIGHBORHOOD GARDEN ASSOCIATION OF PHILADELPHIA

In 1953, Mrs. Bush-Brown founded the Neighborhood Garden Association of Philadelphia fulfilling her dream of beautifying and improving urban spaces with plants. The organization started with two gardens sponsored in seven pilot blocks. By 1961, there were 301 blocks, 15 vacant lot gardens, 12 play areas, 122 4-H (head, heart, hands, health) project gardens, and 1200 doorway gardens in low income housing projects. The program was so successful, it was copied by organizations in cities across the U.S. including in Wilmington, Washington D.C., St. Louis, and Boston. For her efforts, Mrs. Bush-Brown received several prestigious awards and an invitation to speak at the White House. Elizabeth Roosevelt '50 remembers, *"Mrs. Bush-Brown was best of all, teaching about plants and Quakerism by her fine example in helping the underprivileged in Philadelphia."*

STUDENTS WORKING IN CITY GARDENS.

*Hilda Justice Library*

Built in 1951, the library has a beautifully proportioned Reading room and a Rare Book room designed to house a distinguished collection of 16th century Herbals and many other early writings on plants and gardens.

In 1951, a new library was added to the PSHW campus to provide facilities for research and study in horticulture and landscape design. A special rare book room in the library was dedicated to Miss Anna E. Heick, Mrs. Bush-Brown's longtime assistant, to honor her hard work and commitment over the decades. The room contained a fine collection of 16th and 17th century books on gardening, horse husbandry, and herbals. There was also a volume that held color plates of the first botanical drawings done from living plants—including a magnificent collection of flower plates by Mary Vaux Walcott, which was issued by the Smithsonian Institute. The Hilda Justice building is now used for the display of artifacts and preservation of the school's growing collection.

ANNA E. HEICK
(D.1963)

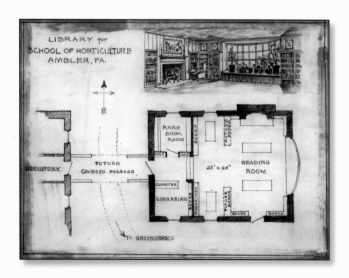

**PHOTOGRAPHS:** (TOP) HILDA JUSTICE MEMORIAL LIBRARY; (CENTER RIGHT) MISS ANNA HEICK, 1940; (BOTTOM LEFT) BLUEPRINT FOR THE HILDA JUSTICE LIBRARY; (BOTTOM RIGHT) STUDENTS WORKING IN THE LIBRARY, 1952; **OPPOSITE PAGE:** (TOP LEFT) THE BIG STORM IN MARCH, 1958, (CENTER) THE FAMOUS MONKEY; (BOTTOM RIGHT) STUDENTS TURNING THE HAY.

# 1958

"In March a heavy wet snow storm brought down many trees and power lines in the region. We were snowed in for several days with no electric or heat. We moved into the student rec room which had a fireplace with our sleeping bags and blankets, and Mr. Hale helped us with firewood. Fortunately the kitchen cooking power was gas, so we still had hot meals. As an Aggie tending the stock was difficult, daylight hours only or by flashlight. Especially difficult was milking the cows by hand—twice a day! After about three days the roads were cleared enough, and, if you had a way, you could go home. Power was not restored on campus for over a week."

—Dusty (Mary Anne Fry)

Nancy Gibbons recalls; *"The BIG SNOW was a challenge for everyday issues; washing hair was made easier by going to the back room of the greenhouse, where the sun had warmed the water in the pipes and also produced warmer air for drying hair... A number of students spent their days in the TV room where there was plenty of daylight and a fireplace to keep them warm. This area was also used by the pet monkey... Eventually wood smoke and monkey smells drove most away. Some went to their rooms and worked by candlelight on the soon due term paper; later turned in with wax drops... Other students who lived nearby went home to family and took as many other students with them as possible. In one home the dining table became a place where multiple portable typewriters were used to work on the term paper... All in all a memorable experience which we all survived... Being the self sufficient young women we were, we came out on the other end with smiles on our faces."*

Just a few weeks after the big snow, the students were notified of a great change to the campus and their campus life. The school would merge with Temple University. The senior class would become the first to graduate with an Associate of Science degree from Temple University. However, for the juniors, there would be a major adjustment. The Agriculture course would be discontinued; the Ag students were given the option to stay on and change their major to Horticulture or Landscape Design. There were only five Ag students; two elected to finish their education elsewhere and three remained as Landscape Design students. Gail Murch, one of the Agriculture students that stayed on to graduate in 1959, remembered how she and her classmates had to cram an entire semester of learning into several weeks during the summer session.

# Diamonds of the Decades (1950–1959)

### HELEN FOSTER '50

After the School of Horticulture, Helen went on to graduate in biology from Whitworth College in Spokane, WA. It was there that she spent summers teaching horticulture therapy at a local hospital, taking patients in the garden and on nature walks for recuperative therapy.

In 1983, she was invited to join a discovery tour of the Galapagos Islands aboard HMS Beagle III as a specialist in Botany. In later years, she was commissioned by the government to complete a study on New Mexican native grasses.

### ELIZABETH HARLAN BREIDENBAUGH '52

Elizabeth remains an active "Aggie" today. She still runs the family dairy farm in Glen Arm, MD, as the fourth generation owner of the 225 acre establishment. She not only manages a herd of registered Holsteins, but also raises all of the feed necessary for them. 100 acres of the farm are reserved for growing vegetables—sweet corn (60 acres), tomatoes, cucumbers, squash and others for farm market. Her family has followed in her footsteps. Her son, Bill works in the dairy, and another son, George, had added a greenhouse to the business and raises bedding plants for spring sales.

### LOIS NICKERSON '51

After her graduation, Lois worked at Phillips Nurseries in Wilmington, DE. She later owned and operated her own nursery, Heritage Gardens, and a florist shop, Kennett Florists. Lois has since chaired a local landscape committee and remains very active in her current community.

### JOAN EASTMAN BENNETT '53

Joan excels as a writer, a landscape designer, and a lecturer. Self-employed in a landscape design business, Joan worked with private home owners and some commercial properties. In Ventnor, NJ, she designed the landscaping around the historic 'Lucy the Elephant.'

Joan has also assisted the school, serving as a field representative; she contacted school guidance counsellors and met with prospective students. In 1987, Joan started a new business venture; Pet Vacation Exchange, Inc.

**PHOTOGRAPHS:** (ABOVE LEFT) THE MUSIC CLUB MEETS IN THE REC ROOM OF THE 1929 DORMITORY, 1956; (ABOVE RIGHT) KATHY MCCABE SHELDON COLLECTS EGGS FROM THE HEN HOUSE IN 1958. **OPPOSITE PAGE:** JUNIOR CLASS OF 1953.

### Jo Davis Malessa '55

Jo worked at Friend's Hospital in Horticulture Therapy, as an assistant to Helen Foster '50. While a student at the school, Jo enjoyed volunteering with the Neighborhood Garden Project.

Jo is still active in the Alumni Association and school events. In 2001, she spoke at the new greenhouse dedication, reminiscing about her days at PSHW.

### Merilyn Caccia Pucillo '57

Merilyn owns and operates a family garden center in New Rochelle, NY, called Cooper's Corner Nursery. Together with her husband, an architect, they do all phases of landscaping. As a student, "Cacci" drove stock cars in local rallies and was known as the "stock car racing master mechanic." She also had a pet snake, which the girls moved from room to room in the dorm to keep the housemother, Mrs. McKinney from doing her daily inspections.

### Janna Bruins '55

Janna worked in the Animal Hospital in Boston where she trained to be a nurse in the general care of animals after her graduation.

She later trained to be a lab technician at Harvard University where she worked in the Dental Research lab caring for the department's white rat colony. She quotes: "I feel that the training I had in Agricultural courses at Ambler has contributed to my subsequent work in labs on animal nutrition and care."

### Monica Moran Brandies '58

Accomplished both as a lecturer and as an author, Monica has written and co-authored 11 books. For over 25 years, she has also written newspaper columns in Ohio, Iowa, and Florida. As a mother of nine, she utilized her growing and canning skills to help feed the family.

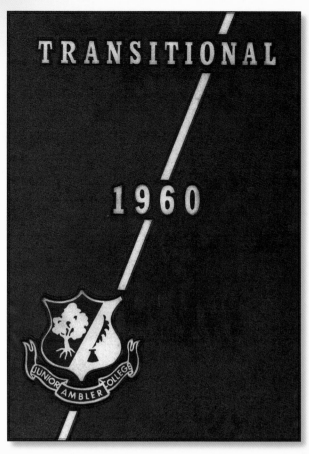

Cover of 1960 Ambler Junior College yearbook.

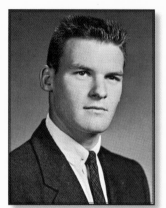

One of the first gentlemen to come to the school, Raymond Shay gained an education and a wife, classmate Nancy Obermayer. Ray worked for Austin Company in Ohio as a landscape gardener. Nancy tended flower gardens, a large vegetable garden, and children.

The other man to graduate in 1960 was Norman MacFarlane. Norman worked with Longwood gardens and was responsible for the tropical greenhouses.

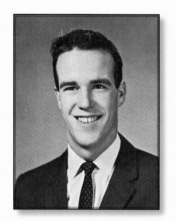

Just as the names changed, so did the logos, several times. The changing logos of the school can be seen: (left) Pennsylvania School of Horticulture for Women, (center) 1959 Transitional, and (right) the Ambler Campus of Temple University.

# A Changing Campus

THE COWS MAKE WAY FOR THE HORSES

On April 22, 1958 it was announced to the student body that the school had merged with Temple University and would be called Ambler Junior College, a division of Temple University. When the merger of PSHW with Temple University was finalized, Mr. John Anthony Brown, Director of Development at Temple, stated that *"the emphasis will remain on horticulture and practical work in greenhouses and gardens. (They would) also maintain the familiar customs and traditions."* Although the traditions remained, the curriculum changed, drastically for some. The Horticulture and Landscape Design programs continued under Temple. Sadly, for lack of funding, the Agriculture Program was terminated in 1958. All of the farm animals and the prized herd of Jersey Cattle were sold off over the summer of 1958, sparing only the horses. For eight more years, the Horse Husbandry program continued as an elective course and the school maintained stables and continued to hold Horse Shows.

The curriculum was not the only thing to change. After 43 years as the Pennsylvania School of Horticulture for Women, the school would become co-ed and be known as Ambler Junior College of Temple University. On June 19, 1958, the first students received diplomas from Ambler Junior College, Temple University, with twenty five graduates in total—10 Landscape Design, 7 Horticulture, and 8 in Agriculture. Following that year, the Alumnae opted to change their name to incorporate newer members, and thus became the Alumnae Association of Ambler Junior College. This name did not last long, and the very next year, it was changed again, this time to the Horticulture Council Ambler Junior College, to distinguish itself from those connected to other colleges within Temple University.

Due to the many administrative changes that occurred in 1958, the graduating class was told that they would not receive their diplomas on the day of graduation, but would have to wait for them in the mail.

Commencement brochures printed for the occasion displayed the title, Ambler Junior College, while the logo was for the School of Horticulture.

TEMPLE·UNIVERSITY

AMBLER·JUNIOR·COLLEGE

THIS·IS·TO·CERTIFY·THAT

MARY·ANNE·BLAIR

HAS·SATISFACTORILY·COMPLETED·THE·PRESCRIBED·COURSE·OF·STUDY·AND UPON·RECOMMENDATION·OF·THE·FACULTY·IS·AWARDED THE·DEGREE·OF

ASSOCIATE·IN·SCIENCE
WITH·HONORS

TOGETHER·WITH·ALL·THE·RIGHTS·AND·PRIVILEGES·APPERTAINING·THERETO GIVEN·AT·PHILADELPHIA·PENNSYLVANIA·JUNE·19·1958

# Timeline...

| 1950 | 1953 | APRIL 22, 1958 | FALL, 1958 |
|---|---|---|---|
| THE SCHOOL RESTRUCTURES THE CURRICULUM TO MEET THE REQUIREMENTS FOR JUNIOR COLLEGE STATUS. IN 1951 IT IS ACCREDITED AS A JUNIOR COLLEGE. | A THIRD YEAR OF STUDY IS OFFERED TO GAIN A CERTIFICATE OF ADVANCED STUDY. | THE PENNSYLVANIA SCHOOL OF HORTICULTURE MERGES WITH TEMPLE UNIVERSITY AND IS RENAMED AMBLER JUNIOR COLLEGE OF TEMPLE UNIVERSITY. | THE FIRST MALE STUDENTS ARE ADMITTED TO AMBLER JUNIOR COLLEGE, TEMPLE UNIVERSITY. |

**PHOTOGRAPHS:** (TOP LEFT) BRIGHT HALL; (TOP RIGHT) CLAIRE WEIR WHITING AND CAROLYN WEINBERG STUDY SEEDLINGS WITH PROFESSOR HANS ZUTTER; (CENTER LEFT) STUDENTS TAKE AN APPLE IDENTIFICATION TEST; (CENTER RIGHT) 1965 DORM COMPLEX; (LOWER LEFT) STUDENTS PLANT SEED POTATOES; (LOWER RIGHT) FLOWER ARRANGING CLASS.

*Timeline...*

### APRIL 27, 1960

DEDICATION OF BRIGHT HALL, NAMED FOR JANE LINN IRWIN BRIGHT, A DEVOTED FRIEND OF PSH. HER DAUGHTER BEQUEATHED A MAJOR PORTION OF THE COST OF THE BUILDING.

### 1961

NEW INSTALLATIONS ADDED TO GREENHOUSE, AN AUTOMATIC MISTING SYSTEM, STEAM STERILIZER, SOIL MIXER, AND THERMOSTAT CONTROLLED VENTS.

### 1963

FIRE DESTROYS DORM! "COTTAGE HALL" IS QUICKLY ESTABLISHED TO HOUSE STUDENTS. DR. EUGENE UDELL BECOMES DEAN OF CAMPUS.

### 1966

THE DAIRY BARN IS CONVERTED FOR LARGE EQUIPMENT STORAGE. AN 80' X 50' ADDITION IS ADDED TO THE OLD RED BARN TO ENLARGE THE GYMNASIUM.

# CHAPTER 7: A New Era for Ambler— 1960's

In 1959, the colonial style Bright Hall was completed. The 18,000 square foot building contained five classrooms, three laboratories, a library and a social center. In addition to Bright Hall, six new dormitories were added to the campus—greatly changing the school atmosphere, as men were finally able to reside on campus. The two dorm complexes each held three wings to provide separate accommodation for 300 male and female students. With the completion of the new dormitories, a strict curfew was imposed on the women, with a house mother and residential advisors in each wing to enforce it. However, these restrictions did not always dissuade the students, who occasionally broke out for late night escapades. One 1966 graduate, Dave Trusal recalls a time when he and several friends decided to go to Kennett Square, *"I lived off campus and had a car, in the very early morning I drove to the girl's dorm and waited outside while the two girls (unnamed) escaped the dorm's lock-down by crawling through a small window above the washing machines in the laundry room."*

Horse husbandry and riding programs all continued as electives for most of the 1960's as did an open show and country meet. It attracted over 100 local riders to a full day of competition in equitation and hunter classes in proper show attire. In 1964, the Ambler Country Meet was combined with the Alumni Harvest Fair for a long September day of competition and purchasing of wares. In following years, the meet was in the Spring with the final show held in May, 1966. The school auctioned off the horses and equipment, after first giving students the option to purchase them. With the sale of the horses, the era of Agriculture at Ambler officially ended.

In 1968, the school experienced the largest enrollment in recent years, with 32 freshmen, 23 of whom were men. That same year, Eugene Udell left to become Vice Provost of Temple University and Dr. John R. Cassidy succeeded him as the Dean of the Ambler Campus.

Claire Weir Whiting '66 recalls the cold days when *"Dean Fisher, who taught "woodies," took us on winter tree identification walks and then back to Wellington Cottage for a hot cider with cinnamon sticks."*

**PHOTOGRAPHS:** (TOP LEFT) STUDENTS HEAD TO BRIGHT HALL FOR CLASS; (ABOVE) 1966 HORSE SHOW WITH DORMITORIES VISIBLE IN THE BACKGROUND; A 1966 HORSE SHOW RIBBON; STUDENTS WEAR THEIR COLLEGE BEANIES; A FRESHMEN REQUIREMENT; (LEFT) WELLINGTON (DEAN'S) COTTAGE.

It was the Fourth of July weekend, 1963, (the students were away for the holiday weekend), when a disaster struck the Ambler campus. A fire broke out in the 1929 dormitory and raged for several hours despite the heroic effort of local fire crews. Luckily, as it was a holiday weekend, no one was caught in the blaze. Sadly though, the intensity of the fire destroyed everything inside, and only the portraits of Jane Bowne Haines and Louise Carter Bush-Brown were saved by the firemen. The residents lost everything and the school lost its beautiful dormitory.

With the fire, not only did the appearance of the campus change, but so did the feel. Students were rehoused at nearby farms or in small cottages built on campus, but with the loss of the beloved dormitory, the school also lost its student camaraderie. Cottage Hall provided a quick solution to the accommodation crisis, but it did not provide the same atmosphere that had led to the formation of lifelong friendships. After the fire the school took more than twenty years to fully mend the extensive damage.

Phyllis Woerner Deisroth '40 returned to the campus to view the damage; *"Today I walked through the ashes. I told myself I was dreaming, that this couldn't be so… I walked around to the garden side to view the ruins. Surely it couldn't be any worse. But it was… The sweet savor of the Boxwoods filled my nostrils—that old familiar scent. Unashamedly, the tears fell."*

—*Pen & Trowel* Fall-Winter, 1963

Toni Tosco, a student at the time of the fire, wrote to *Pen & Trowel; "We students who lost personal possessions in the fire realized for the first time that one never knows when disaster might strike. Suddenly, we had lost all clothing, books, notes and a few items of sentimental value. The loss of our books and notes was a great inconvenience, since we had to continue with the summer session…We were left with just memories…We realized that sometimes all we really have is within ourselves. With courage and tremendous effort, we began anew."*

**PHOTOGRAPHS:** (ABOVE LEFT) NEWSPAPER CLIPPING FROM AMBLER GAZETTE, JULY 5 1963; NEWSPAPER ARTICLE FROM PHILADELPHIA INQUIRER JULY 8, 1963; (TOP RIGHT) PHOTOGRAPHS OF THE DORMITORY AFTER THE FIRE; COTTAGE HALL.
**OPPOSITE PAGE:** (MIDDLE) A RIBBON FROM THE 1934 HARVEST HOME; (TOP RIGHT) 1968 HARVEST FAIR POSTER; (CENTER LEFT) 1953 PLANT SALE POSTER;(LOWER RIGHT) POEM BY HELEN PFAFFINGER IN 1960 'WISE ACRES;' (BOTTOM) CROWDS OF SHOPPERS AT THE 1968 PLANT SALE.

# Fall Harvest Fair and Plant Sales

Throughout the decades, the school held many Harvest Fairs and Plant Sales that were designed to bring in revenue to help the school and campus.

The school's famous apple cider was often a popular purchase at the Fall Harvest Fair, along with the canned foods, jams, and cured meats. The flower arranging booth sold dried flowers, grasses, pods and cones for bouquet and wreath making. Horticultural students propagated and divided house plants to sell. A local family would lend their pony for pony rides and a school horse was used on a lead line for older children. Strong winds nearly blew the Harvest Fair away in 1968, the last year that it was held.

In the early days of the Plant Sale, local estate owners would come with their gardeners and chauffeurs to select plants for their gardens. Any plants intended for the school's use had to be hidden and guarded so they were not mistakenly sold. At the opening of the sale, customers would dash to the cold frames for the prized delphiniums, foxgloves and canterbury bells. The annual sale thrived for many years, especially during the 1960's when thousands of attendees braved the weather and lined up to purchase the students' well-cultivated wares.

An Ode to the Plant Sale
by Helen Pfaffinger

'Twas the night before the
plant sale
and all through the dorm
All the students were stirring
to prepare for the morn.
All the seedlings were watered,
all snug in their beds,
While visions of stampedes
danced through our heads.

*Timeline...*

### 1948
THE FIRST HARVEST "HOME" IS STAGED BY THE ALUMNI AND COLLEGE. AFTER NO FAIR IN '54, THE '55 FAIR IS BOOKED AS A "COMEBACK" BUT HEAVY RAINS RELEGATE IT TO THE DORMITORY.

### 1966
PRISCILLA-GENE WEST SHAFFER '60 ADDS A SMALL FLOWER SHOW TO THE HARVEST FAIR, INVITING LOCAL GARDEN CLUB PARTICIPATION.

### 1967
THE HARVEST FAIR AND PHS FALL FLOWER SHOW COMBINE ON THE AMBLER CAMPUS. AN ESTIMATED 1000 PEOPLE ATTEND; A LECTURE PROGRAM WAS THE ADDED ATTRACTION.

### 1968
THE JOINT FALL EVENT IS HELD AGAIN. DESPITE EXTREMELY WINDY CONDITIONS, A RECORD 4000 PEOPLE ATTEND.

# Diamonds of the Decades (1960–1969)

### JULIE MORRIS '60

Julie worked for Ernesta Ballard managing Valley Gardens. She continued at Temple earning a degree in Urban Sociology. She was a librarian at Pennsylvania Horticultural Society and assisted with Neighborhood Garden Association. Julie served as alumni association treasurer.

### BARBARA MESSNER '60

After graduating from Temple Ambler, Barbara worked as a floral designer. She became an assistant to William Hixon at Hixon's well known Floral Design School, and has represented Hixon's at worldwide trade shows.

### FREDERICK N. SCHROEDER '61

In 1991, "Fritz" returned to Ambler for his 30th reunion with an interest in the garden restoration project under John Collins. Fritz became an avid supporter of the project, contributing time, material, money, and labor; *"I am happy to be able to give something back to the institution that inspired me."*

### TONI TOSCO '64

From September '66–April '67, Toni worked in Costa Rica as an International Farm Youth Exchange student. Later, Toni became one of the garden supervisors at Leonard J. Buck Garden, Far Hills, NJ.

PHOTOGRAPH: (ABOVE) IN 1992, GRADUATES FROM 1964, '65, '66, AND '67 REUNITED BY THE FOUNTAIN IN THE LOUISE BUSH-BROWN FORMAL GARDENS TO REMEMBER THEIR FORMER CLASSMATE CAROLYN WEINBERG '66.

> *"Looking back, my time at Ambler was a fabulous experience... The program was strong academically but also practical: you learned the basics of planting, arboriculture, and horticulture—you got your hands dirty..."*
>
> —Bill Mifflin '66

### GARY KOLLER '65

After his graduation, Gary became a medic during the Vietnam war. When he returned, Gary completed the Longwood Public Gardens program and worked at the Arnold Arboretum of Harvard University as supervisor of the living collection. He has since started his own design firm, Koller & Associates. Gary won a gold medal from the Massachusetts Horticulture Society.

### WILLIAM MIFFLIN '66

Bill has never left Ambler. He first graduated in 1966 with an AS in Ornamental Horticulture. Later, Bill received a BS in Recreation Management 1968, and then a Master of Education in Recreational Administration in 1986. Bill worked for the Philadelphia Fairmount Park Commission and advanced to executive director. Bill now serves on the Ambler Campus Board of Visitors.

### GEORGE & PAT (HANNAHS) MOORE '66

Pat and George met while students at Temple University Ambler. After graduation, the couple joined George's family's business, Moore's Farm Market & Garden Center located in Bayville, NJ.

While writing this book, we were saddened to learn of George's death. A note from Pat reminded us how he loved working with the family, enjoyed his customers, and always said, *"take time to stop and smell the roses."*

### CLAIRE WEIR WHITING '66

Claire has a passion for Ambler and served as President of the Alumni Association, holding the group together through some difficult times.

With both banking and bookkeeping experience, Claire was instrumental in transferring alumni funds into two endowed scholarships, the James and Louise Bush-Brown Scholarship and the Horticultural/Landscape Alumni Association Scholarship to Temple University.

FRESHMAN STUDENTS at Temple University's Ambler Campus held the 9th Annual Flower Arranging Show in connection with their flower arranging class on July 22, in Bright Hall on the Ambler Campus. Three Philadelphians were among the 19 students participating. Left to right: Claire Weir, 7642 Rugby St., William Mifflin, 8006 Crispin St., and Carolyn Weinberg, 403 W. Mt. Airy Ave. Miss Weir took first prize in greetings, an arrangement for a hall table, which she is holding. This winning entry in this category was also judged "best in the show." Miss Weinberg took a second prize in From Dawn to Dusk, an arrangement using one kind of flower from bud to full bloom, on the far right.

**PHOTOGRAPHS:** (LEFT) 1966 CLASS PHOTO; (RIGHT) A NEWSPAPER CLIPPING ABOUT THE 9TH ANNUAL FLOWER ARRANGING SHOW IN 1965 AT WHICH AMBLER FRESHMEN CLAIRE WEIR, WILLIAM MIFFLIN, AND CAROLYN WEINBERG WON SEVERAL AWARDS.

PREMIERE SEASON
TEMPLE
UNIVERSITY
MUSIC FESTIVAL
& INSTITUTE

1968

On August 4, 1968, after the conclusion of its first successful six week Music Festival season, the Ambler campus returned to its normal symphony of nature. During the festival visitors were serenaded by the sounds of famous musicians, including Benny Goodman, Ella Fitzgerald and the Chamber Symphony of Philadelphia conducted by Anshel Brusilow.

Dr. David L. Stone, who was then the Dean of the College of Music, said that he hoped this festival would come to rival similar events such as Tanglewood in Massachusetts and the Hopkins Center Festival at Dartmouth College. Attendees of the event agreed with Dr. Stone and thought that they may have just witnessed the start of what could become one of the best known music festivals in the country. Unfortunately after thirteen delightful seasons the festival closed.

# CHAPTER 8: *Modern History: 1970–1999*

The campus continued to evolve during the latter years of this historical century and the student population grew exponentially with many men joining the ranks. Between 1970 and 1982, many new buildings were added to the Ambler campus, including a larger library, dining facilities, Widener Hall and Dixon Hall, two fiberglass greenhouses, and a student center. Widener Hall was opened in 1978 with funding from the Widener Foundation. Dixon Hall, completed in 1982, was built to replace the 1929 dorm with landscaping at the back of the building extending into the Formal Gardens.

With the growing student body, it became apparent that developing baccalaureate degrees was essential for growth of the school. In the 1980's, Department Chair Dr. Elizabeth Sluzis oversaw the curriculum committee for Undergraduate and Graduate courses. The graduating class of 1990 was the first to receive four year degrees in Horticulture, Landscape Design, and Landscape Architecture. The Landscape Architecture program was also given accreditation in 1991 by the American Society of Landscape Architects.

## AMBLER CAMPUS IN 1973

The "Pit" where the 1929 dormitory had stood is still visible. In 1975, students in Horticulture and Landscape Design worked together to clean out the "Pit" for landscaping. The East Wing, not completely destroyed in the fire, was also converted for classroom space.

1. 1973 library
2. Bright Hall
3. 1965 dormitory complex
4. Cottage Halls
5. The "Pit"

6. Hilda Justice
7. Greenhouses
8. The barn, now the gym
9. Administration building

**PHOTOGRAPHS:** (TOP RIGHT) FACULTY MEMBERS BREAK GROUND FOR DIXON HALL; (ABOVE) A 1973 VIEW OF CAMPUS.
**OPPOSITE PAGE:** (LEFT) PROGRAM COVER FOR THE 1968 MUSIC FESTIVAL; (RIGHT) ONE OF THE MANY CLASSICAL MUSIC CONCERTS HELD; (LOWER LEFT) AN AERIAL VIEW OF THE CAMPUS SET UP WITH TENTS FOR THE MUSIC FESTIVAL; (TOP) STUDENTS PLAYING GUITAR ON THE CAMPUS GROUNDS.

## Timeline...

| JUNE 1970 | 1971 | 1973 | 1979 |
|---|---|---|---|
| ALUMNI SELECT A NEW LOGO, A TROWEL AND STEM OF WHEAT, DESIGNED BY LINDA WALZ '70. MR. BETTES WORKS ON A DESIGN FOR LOUISE STEIN FISHER MEMORIAL GARDEN. | DR. SIDNEY HALPERN BECOMES DIRECTOR. HE LATER BECOMES DEAN IN 1975, HE STAYS 9 YEARS AND IS SUCCEEDED BY JAMES BLACKHURST IN 1984. | THE NEW LIBRARY IS BUILT WITH PLANS TO OPEN IN FALL. MRS. BUSH-BROWN DIES IN DECEMBER 1973 AND THE FORMAL GARDENS ARE DEDICATED TO HER ON JUNE 23, 1974. | VIOLA K. ANDERS RETIRES AFTER 25 YEARS WITH THE COLLEGE. ALUMNI ASSSOCIATION GIVES AWARD IN HER NAME. |

During the seventies and eighties, the school laid the foundations for a future focus on environmental sustainability through activities such as tree planting, continued involvement in city garden blocks, and the development of the school grounds. In 1992, John Collins became Department Chair of Horticulture and Landscape Design. Under his leadership, assisted by Stephanie Cohen, the existing gardens were refurbished and new ones were planned. In 1998 Stephanie Cohen and Rudy Keller redesigned and replanted the formal perennial gardens. The campus was officially recognized as an Arboretum in the year 2000.

**PHOTOGRAPHS:** (TOP ROW L-R) STUDENTS PLANTING TREES ON CAMPUS IN THE 1970'S; STUDENTS DEMONSTRATE THE CAMPUS' GROWING INTEREST IN THE ENVIRONMENT; A STUDENT WATERS THE FORMAL GARDENS, DIXON HALL CAN BE SEEN IN THE BACKGROUND; (BOTTOM ROW L-R) A STUDENT TENDS THE TULIPS IN THE FORMAL GARDENS, 1970'S; STEPHANIE COHEN (ON LEFT) AND JOHN COLLINS (ON RIGHT) POSE WITH SCULPTOR S. JOSEPH WINTER AT THE INSTALLATION OF THE HERB GARDEN; THE CUTTING GARDENS, IN THE BACKGROUND IS HILDA JUSTICE AND THE REMAINS OF THE EAST WING OF THE 1929 DORMITORY - CONVERTED FOR CLASSROOM SPACE, 1975; (BOTTOM) 1990 COURTYARD GARDEN.

*Timeline...*

### 1986

OLYMPIC POOL, LIGHTED BASKETBALL COURT AND TENNIS COURTS ARE ALL ADDED. JIM PULLI RETIRES AS GROUNDS TECHNICIAN AFTER 30 YEARS.

### JUNE 10, 1990

ALUMNI ASSOCIATION DONATES A NEW BRONZE STATUE FOR THE GARDEN FOUNTAIN, THE SCULPTOR IS S. JOSEPH WINTER.

### 1990

MONEY GIFTED FOR COURTYARD GARDEN BY THE GENERAL ALUMNI ASSOCIATION OF TEMPLE. DR. HANS ZUTTER RETIRES AFTER 35 YEARS.

### 1997

CORRINE CALDWELL BECOMES DEAN; INITIATES CONTINUING EDUCATION CLASSES. DR. GEORGE MANAKER RETIRES AFTER 35 YEARS.

# Philadelphia Flower Shows

At the 1967 Philadelphia Flower Show, teacher Viola K. Anders and student Gloria Dreisbach arranged potted flowers for the school's California patio inspired exhibit for which they won several awards.  As the Flower Show grew in size and prestige so did the complexity of the displays. Starting in 1972, the school recognized its strength in the environmental focus with an exhibit by Vincent C. McDermott for the theme: "The Environment: How it Affects Plants." Mr. Hans A. Zutter and Dr. George Manaker supplied hundreds of plants for the exhibit.  These plants were all subjected to a variety of controlled changes in water, air, light, nutrition, temperature, nutrition, and gravity in order to show the effects of environmental changes. For their efforts, they were given  the Flower Show Award by PHS and Bulkley Medal of the Garden Club of America for "an exhibit of special merit and/or educational value."

Over the next few decades, the school took home many more awards for their exhibits. As the school's focus leaned more towards environmental sustainability, so too did their Flower Show displays, which were mainly on nature and the environment. In 2001, a green roof was built on the Ambler campus using the flower show model, and both the "Nature Nurtures" and "Sustainable Wetlands" exhibits were used as foundations for gardens in the Ambler Arboretum. In 1987 and 2005, the school's participants chose to use the opportunity to display the Ambler campus' proud history, first under the title "Dig It, Do It" and then as "Progressive Women" for which they took home the "Best of Show" in 2005.

**PHOTOGRAPHS:** (TOP RIGHT) 1967 VIOLA K. ANDERS RECREATES A CALIFORNIA PATIO, (MIDDLE) IN 1988 PRISCILLA-GENE WEST SHAFFER '60 TOOK HOME AN AWARD FOR THE SCHOOL; (CENTER LEFT) 2005 EXHIBIT EXPLORES THE SCHOOL'S HISTORY, MIRRORING THE 1987 FLOWER SHOW EXHIBIT "DIG IT, DO IT"; (CENTER) LAUREN DUBS '08 PUTS THE PLANTS INTO THE "NATURE NURTURES" DISPLAY, WHICH WAS LATER USED AS A BASIS FOR THE ERNESTA BALLARD HEALING GARDEN; (CENTER RIGHT) THE GREEN ROOF EXHIBIT, LATER RECREATED IN A FULL SIZE MODEL ON THE CAMPUS IN 2005; (LEFT) DR. GEORGE MANAKER, VINCENT MCDERMOTT, AND HANS ZUTTER PUT THE FINISHING TOUCHES ON THE 1972 EXHIBIT.

*Timeline...*

### 1999

SOPHIA WISNIEWSKA BECOMES DEAN. JAMES W. HILTY FOLLOWS IN 2006. WILLIAM E. PARSHALL BECOMES EXECUTIVE DIRECTOR OF AMBLER CAMPUS IN 2010

### 2000

CENTER FOR SUSTAINABLE COMMUNITIES OPENS WITH DR. JEFFREY FEATHERSTONE AS DIRECTOR.

### 2003

SUSTAINABLE WETLAND GARDEN DEVELOPED AS THE RESULT OF 1997 FLOWER SHOW EXHIBIT AND GENEROUS SUPPORT FROM PETER G. SCHLOTTERER, TU '49.

### 2005

THE GREEN ROOF IS DEDICATED AS PART OF AMBLER'S SUSTAINABLE COMMUNITIES. IN 2006, THE LEARNING CENTER IS OPENED WITH STATE FUNDING OF $17 MILLION.

# CHAPTER 9: *The New Millenium*

With the new millenium came new changes for Temple Ambler, including yet another name change for the campus to Ambler College of Temple University. The campus was also recognized for its historical significance with an historical marker dedicated to commemorate the school's early initiatives in Horticulture, Landscape Design and Agriculture, especially in regard to women's education. Today the school has continued to progress with changes to the curriculum to adapt to current interests in Sustainable Development, Community and Regional Planning, and the growing fields of Landscape Architecture and Design.

In 2000, thanks to Stephanie Cohen and Phil Albright, the campus was officially recognized as an Arboretum. In that same year, the Center for Sustainable Communities was established; and in 2001 the school was awarded a $1.5 million federal grant. The "green" focus expanded further when the school became known as the School of Environmental Design (SED) in the College of Liberal Arts (CLA) in 2009, which incorporated the Departments of Community and Regional Planning, Landscape Architecture and Horticulture, and the Center for Sustainable Communities.

As technology burst onto the scene, the Learning Center was built to allow students and faculty to keep pace. It quickly became used for campus education and community outreach with the classrooms and an auditorium. Even with the modern additions, the uniqueness of the campus remains; with the old farm house—Haines House, the matching classroom building—now home of the Administration, the barn and silo—now the gymnasium, all still being enhanced with the lovely gardens of the Arboretum. It is a place for students to learn the variety of occupations offered in Horticulture, Landscape Design, Landscape Architecture, and regional planning; to succeed in their chosen professions.

**PHOTOGRAPHS:** (TOP) HISTORIC MARKER DEDICATION, 2002; (ABOVE LEFT) 2008 FACULTY; (ABOVE RIGHT) THE DISPLAY GARDENS, WITH BARN AND WOMAN'S NATIONAL FARM & GARDEN VISITOR CENTER. **OPPOSITE PAGE:** (TOP LEFT) GREEN ROOF, DEDICATED IN 2005; (TOP RIGHT) STUDENT'S RECYCLED PAPER PROJECT, EARTHFEST, APRIL 2011; (CENTER LEFT) NEW GREENHOUSE COMPLEX, DEDICATED FALL, 2001; (CENTER RIGHT) THE LEARNING CENTER DEDICATION, OCTOBER 11, 2006; (BOTTOM LEFT) STUDENTS VISIT THE CAMPUS DURING OPEN HOUSE, OCTOBER 20, 2006; (BOTTOM RIGHT) GEORGE WHITING TEACHING HERBACEOUS CLASS IN THE ALL AMERICA SELECT DISPLAY GARDEN.

## GALLERY OF SUCCESS, AMBLER

**2001**
WILLIAM E. MIFFLIN '66
INEZ O'MALLEY '79

**2002**
CHRISTOPHER PALMER '02
ERNESTA BALLARD '54

**2003**
JANE PEPPER '74
RODNEY BIERHUIZEN '02

**2004**
HOLLY HARMER SHIMIZU '74
DONNA M. SWANSEN '81

**2005**
JOHN J. BLANDY '75
J. JOSEPH BLANDY '00

**2006**
FREDERICK N. SCHROEDER '61
SHAREE SOLOW '03

**2007**
MARY ANNE BLAIR FRY '58
JAMES KAUFMANN '94

**2008**
KEN LEROY '84
MONICA MORAN BRANDIES '58

**2009**
ALISON RIFE THORNTON '03
PHILIP R. ALBRIGHT '86

**2010**
JONATHAN WRIGHT '06

## FOUNDERS' AWARD RECIPIENTS

**2002** STEPHANIE COHEN '56

**2003** CAROLYN COREY JARIN '46

**2004** PHILIP R. ALBRIGHT '86

**2005** JANE G. PEPPER '74

**2006** DONNA M. SWANSEN '81

**2007** JENNY ROSE CAREY '03

**2008** MARY ANNE BLAIR FRY '58

**2009** PAULA DUMAS SOLOMON '02

**2010** CLAIRE WEIR WHITING '66

**PHOTOGRAPHS:** (TOP LEFT) DEAN SOPHIA WISNIEWSKA, ERNESTA BALLARD AND JANE PEPPER (WITH HISTORICAL MARKER); (TOP RIGHT) MONICA MORAN BRANDIES AND KEN LEROY; (SECOND ROW) STEPHANIE COHEN; JAMES KAUFMAN; JOSEPH BLANDY; HOLLY SHIMIZU; (BOTTOM ROW) RODNEY BIERHUIZEN; DONNA SWANSEN; BRAD AND ALISON RIFE THORNTON.

# *This page is dedicated to the men and women...*

## ...WHO WORKED, TAUGHT, AND STUDIED AT THE SCHOOL OF HORTICULTURE FOR WOMEN AND TEMPLE UNIVERSITY AMBLER.

**PHOTOGRAPHS:** (TOP, L-R) MRS. LUSKY, MR. STOVER, GEORGE AND NELLIE BULLOCK, MR. AND MRS. BUSH-BROWN; (MIDDLE L-R) RICK RAY, BALDEV LAMBA, PRISCILLA-GENE WEST SHAFFER; (BOTTOM LEFT) MR. WILLIAM HALE JR, MR. WILLIAM HALE, MR. EARL ROBERTS, MR. JAMES PULLI, MR. ANGELO PULLI; (BOTTOM RIGHT) SEATED: MR. MATZA, MISS. ANDERS, MRS. FISHER, MRS. BUSH-BROWN, MR. ZUTTER, STANDING: MR. THOMAS, MR. MITCHELL, MR. FRENCH, MR. BUSH-BROWN, MR. CADWALDER, DR. SWARTLEY.

**PHOTOGRAPHS:** (CLOCKWISE FROM ABOVE) ALUMNAE OF THE PENNSYLVANIA SCHOOL OF HORTICULTURE ATTEND THE HISTORIC MARKER DEDICATION CEREMONY IN 2002; ALUMNI FROM 1948 AND '58 WITH ALUMNI PRESIDENT ALISON THORNTON AND AMBLER ARBORETUM DIRECTOR JENNY ROSE CAREY, 2009; THE CLASS OF 1948 AT THEIR 50TH REUNION IN 1998.

**PHOTOGRAPHS:** (TOP) A VIEW OF THE PAVILIONS IN THE FORMAL GARDENS, SUMMER 2007. (SECOND ROW, L-R) MERRILL MILLER '72; MICHAEL WILLIAMS WITH GUS CAREY; CHRIS AND CLA DEAN TERESA SOUFAS; ROBERT HALPERN '84. (THIRD ROW L-R) RON MCKNIGHT '70; WILLIAM '66 AND SALLY MIFFLIN, PHIL '86 AND BARBARA ALBRIGHT, KATHY AND DEAN JAMES HILTY, MAUREEN AND BILL THOMPSON; BARRY CYPHERS; (FOURTH ROW L-R) KEN LAWRENCE, WILLIAM PARSHALL, VICKIE MCGARVEY, JANET AND LEW KLEIN; ANN LAUGHLIN '05 AND KIMBERLY LOCK '07; CAROL AND RICK COLLIER.

# Ambler Arboretum

The land that today comprises the arboretum was in 1911 the McAlanon farm. Adjoining parcels of farmland were added later. The main formal gardens of the arboretum are clustered around the buildings, but other interesting plant specimens are found throughout the 187 acre campus. The arboretum is a teaching garden that from the beginning of the Pennsylvania School of Horticulture for Women was the site of practical learning for students. Today's students continue to use the gardens as an outdoor classroom. The arboretum is open from dawn to dusk all year and is free of charge.

From the beginning of the school, the girls and faculty members designed and installed gardens. One of the first gardens was behind Haines House, next to Rose Cottage. It was a Colonial Revival rose garden with boxwood lining the paths. As buildings were added, other gardens evolved.

The centerpiece of the designed gardens is the historic formal perennial garden, originally on axis with the dormitory building, now aligned with Dixon Hall. The Albright winter garden and the native formal garden flank this garden. Below the formal garden, towards Meetinghouse Road, is the Woodland garden. The Colibraro conifer garden and the Ernesta Ballard Healing Garden are located across Albright walk, near the greenhouse. Other gardens include the Louise Stine Fisher Garden, the Viola Anders herb garden and the sustainable wetland garden.

### Jenny Rose Carey

Jenny Rose Carey became the Director of the Ambler Arboretum of Temple University in 2005. Since her arrival, three new gardens have been designed and dedicated and an irrigation system has been installed.
Jenny lectures to groups across the world on a variety of subjects that celebrate the gardens and their rich history. She works with Alumni and friends of the Arboretum to bring visitors to the gardens and to secure donations to maintain this important site.

**PHOTOGRAPHS:** (TOP RIGHT) MEMBERS OF THE 2010 BOARD OF VISITORS AND AMBLER ARBORETUM ADVISORY BOARD—PHOTO BY NANCY TIRRELL PARAVANO; (ABOVE RIGHT) THE AMBLER ARBORETUM ADVISORY BOARD AND HORTICULTURE STAFF WITH "BIG RED" THE OLD RED OAK NEAR COTTAGE HALL; (BACKGROUND) THE BELL TOWER LEADING INTO THE GARDENS.

**Stephanie Cohen '81** *Perennial Diva*

Stephanie was founding Director of the Arboretum. She taught at Ambler for over twenty years and is now a well known author and lecturer.

VIOLA K. ANDERS (ON RIGHT)

Stephanie Cohen, founding director of the Ambler Arboretum and long time faculty member designed the **Viola K. Anders Herb Garden** which is tucked at the side of Dixon Hall. Viola was a much loved faculty member. Alumni wanting to honor her, donated money to dedicate the garden in her name. The herbs that require full sun are located in three quarters of this garden. The fourth quarter has shade loving herbs located under a yew bush. The enclosed space provides an ideal place to appreciate the diverse aromas of fragrant herbs. Students can learn about the plants that for millennia have been used by humans for cooking and flavoring dishes, making and dyeing cloth, scenting their homes and providing medicine. Nearby is the Hilda Justice building, where Mrs. Bush-Brown kept her collection of rare books. Although no longer a library, the Hilda Justice is now the site of the Memorabilia Collection for the campus.

"Beyond the garden lies the woodland where the Senior Students, as a part of the Major work in Floriculture, have developed a garden of native plants. Under the sheltering branches of the hemlocks and the birches many rare and lovely wild flowers have been naturalized."

—1933 Prospectus

The path through the woodland used to lead to the little outdoor theater where many May Day Festivals were held during the years of PSHW. In 1991, azaleas were planted in the woodland as a memorial to Carolyn Weinberg '66. Today the woodland path is still a peaceful walk especially with the blooming of the Spring bulbs and Trillium.

**PHOTOGRAPHS:** (CENTER LEFT) VIOLA ANDERS RECEIVES AN AWARD AT THE 1965 PHILADELPHIA FLOWER SHOW; (TOP RIGHT) VIOLA ANDERS HERB GARDEN; (BOTTOM LEFT INSET) STUDENTS PLANTING ALONG THE WOODLAND PATH, 1935 PROSPECTUS; (BOTTOM LEFT) THE WOODLAND PATH TODAY.

JOHN COLLINS

During his career at Ambler, John Collins provided much inspiration and support for the restoration and beautification of the school grounds. Together with his son John R. he crafted the "East Gate" structures in 1996 to provide a welcoming entrance to visitors of the Ambler Campus. Nearly three decades after their destruction in the dorm fire, the grounds of the former Eastern Cherry Allée were finally recovered under his leadership, and turned into a Native Plant Garden in 1994. This garden is now a showcase for the use of native plants in a formal setting, with a new allée of sour gum, *Nyssa sylvatica*, to provide the shade necessary for the collection of native herbaceous and woody plants to thrive.

**The Sustainable Wetland Garden** is located behind Cottage Hall. This garden was installed in 1997 and drew inspiration from a Philadelphia Flower Show exhibit. Edgar David was the faculty member who led the development of this self sufficient garden. The naturally low-lying area receives drainage water from surrounding buildings and the Bright Hall Quad providing a wet area for plants that favor these conditions. Plants used in this garden were grown from locally collected seed. A solar panel powers water flow over an aerial aqueduct to a fountain. The path is a combination of boardwalk and permeable pebble paving with concrete paving slabs, made by the students, that incorporate cullet, a crushed, recycled glass. This environmentally friendly garden is used to teach why and how we need to design gardens to allow and encourage infiltration of rainwater back into our ground water.

**PHOTOGRAPHS:** (TOP CENTER) NATIVE PLANT GARDEN; (TOP RIGHT) EASTERN CHERRY ALLÉE AS IT EXISTED BEFORE THE FIRE; (BOTTOM LEFT) FOUNTAIN IN THE SUSTAINABLE WETLAND; (BOTTOM RIGHT) CENTRAL FOUNTAIN AREA OF THE SUSTAINABLE WETLAND GARDEN.

LOUISE STEIN FISHER '51

This garden is located at the end of the Albright Winter Garden and is named for **Louise Stein Fisher**. Louise had been in the Marine Corps as a Woman Reserve when she discovered a love of trees and decided to study at the School of Horticulture. Following her graduation she worked at Rodale Press and Star Roses before returning as Dean of Women. She continued to work at Ambler after the transition. After Louise died, Alumni and friends donated money to dedicate this garden in her name on June 12th, 1971. The garden features conifers and a Japanese Maple that surround a gathering area of benches. At the end of the garden there is a vibrant show of tropical plants during the growing season.

**The Colibraro Conifer Garden** located next to the Greenhouse, was dedicated in honor of the Colibraro family in 2010. The plant material was donated by the Colibraros and provides an ideal place to learn about the diversity of coniferous plants. The student can study the names, habit, color and structure of the different trees and shrubs. The bowl-like setting with large boulders provides a gathering spot for groups or individuals.

**PHOTOGRAPHS:** (TOP LEFT) LOUISE STEIN FISHER MEMORIAL GARDEN, 2011; (CENTER RIGHT) LOUISE STEIN FISHER MEMORIAL GARDEN WHEN IT WAS FIRST PLANTED, 1971; (ABOVE) THE COLIBRARO BROTHERS AT THE DEDICATION OF THEIR GARDEN IN 2010 AND THE COLIBRARO CONIFER GARDEN, 2010—PHOTOS BY NANCY TIRRELL PARAVANO.

**The Albright Winter Garden** designed by Mara Baird, was named in 2008, in honor of Barbara and Phil Albright, longtime supporters of the Ambler Arboretum. This garden was the site of the Western Cherry Allee until the dormitory fire damaged the trees. Now the secluded space, surrounded by hedges is the perfect setting for plants that show interest during the gardening off-season. From the fall display of berries, through the fragrant witch hazels and tiny early spring bulbs, students and visitors learn about plants that are the stars of the winter garden. The Japanese Umbrella Pine, Camellia and Crepe Myrtle are older specimens that have performed well in this garden.

BARBARA AND PHIL ALBRIGHT '86

ERNESTA BALLARD '54

**The Healing Garden** was dedicated in June, 2009, to honor an esteemed alumna Ernesta Ballard. Ernesta recalled her time at PSHW as, *"Simply something nice for women to do when I was a student. Now it's career-oriented. And there are men."* Ernesta went on to become the first female President of the Pennsylvania Horticultural Society in addition to writing several books, the first being GARDEN IN YOUR HOUSE, published in 1958. Faculty member Pauline Hurley-Kurtz, students and horticulture staff cleared a site of invasive plants before designing and installing this garden as a full size replica of the 'Nature Nurtures' 2006 Philadelphia Flower Show exhibit. The healing garden contains a central labyrinth of creeping lemon thyme enclosed within the stone walls of a carefully engineered rain garden that draws its water from the roof of Dixon Hall. The water flows through a series of swales before it gradually seeps back into the ground and is absorbed by the plants.

PAULINE HURLEY-KURTZ

**PHOTOGRAPHS:** (MIDDLE LEFT) ALBRIGHT WINTER GARDEN IN SUMMER; (MIDDLE RIGHT) ALBRIGHT WINTER GARDEN IN FALL; (LEFT ERNESTA BALLARD HEALING GARDEN.

## A quote from Mrs. Bush-Brown on the event of the school's 50th anniversary:

"Throughout the years, the School has strived to offer sound instruction in horticulture, landscape design and related subjects; and to prepare its graduates well for the positions in their chosen fields. But its aim has been to do more than this. It has sought to develop in the students a sense of enduring values, an awareness of beauty, and an appreciation of the fine things of life.

The beauty which has surrounded them has touched their lives deeply and will always remain in their hearts. This is the way it has been in the past. This is the way we hope it will continue to be in the future for the many students who will frequent this campus in the years to come."

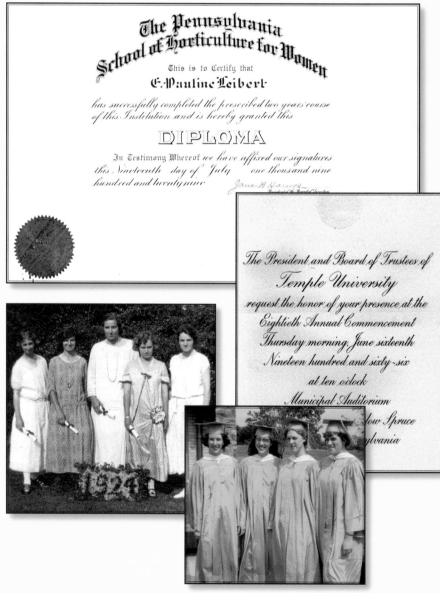

**PHOTOGRAPHS:** (TOP TO BOTTOM) 1916, 1943, 1958, 1970, 2008; (TOP RIGHT) 1924 DIPLOMA AND 1966 GRADUATION INVITATION; (ABOVE LEFT) 1924 CLASS; (ABOVE RIGHT) 1966 CLASS.